Aurora to Ariel

the motorcycling life of

J. W. Graham Oates

a pioneer Manx motorcyclist

by
Bill Snelling

cover illustrations by
Chris Corlett

cover design by
Ruth Sutherland

Amulree Publications

J. W. Graham Oates 1897 - 1972

Contents

Foreword

It is a particular pleasure to write the foreword to a book about a personal friend. As the narrative records, my wife and I first enjoyed the friendship of Graham Oates when we lived in Germany.

Hamburg was an extraordinary place in the period 1947-19 and, no dount, many unlikely relationships were formed amongst the British expatriate population - both Service and civilian. In that curious society Col. Oates was a leading figure in the Control Commission and I was embarking on my broadcasting career with the British Forces Network. We remained in touch following our return to the UK but, as this book reveals, that was probably the least eventful period of a remarkably adventurous life.

What Bill Snelling also reveals are many fascinating and little-known details of the saga of the motor-cycle in the Isle of Man as well as the unusual achievements, both at home and abroad, of one who was proud to be a Manxman, and a credit in every way to his place of birth.

Raymond Baxter, Henley on Thames

Raymond Baxter (center, rear) with Graham and friends, Moose Lodge, Baldrine

Foreword to revised edition

It is a pleasure to have been asked to write this foreword, and I must thank Bill Snelling for bringing my father's motorcycling career to public attention, and indeed for enlightening me about the many of his accomplishments of which I had little or no knowledge.

One of my early memories of my father is my first ever day on a motorcycle. I was 14, and he decided that it was time that I had my first lesson. The bike was a James 125 with a three-speed hand change, and we went to a grassy hill near Glenmaye. After giving me a few tips, he more or less told me to "have a go", and he seemed mightily pleased with my efforts as he was heard to say, "... like a duck to water." He further encouraged me towards competition riding in later years, and always advocated the amateur approach of preparing one's equipment oneself, as far as possible, which was a philosophy that I followed throughout my competitive career racing a Lotus Europa.

I was born in 1933, but sadly my father spoke very little about his career in later years, which meant that I was largely unaware of his earlier life, especially his Canadian adventures. My mother married my father in 1930, having sailed over from the Island that year, and she no doubt encouraged him during that period and back home.

Since the publications of this book's first edition in 1993, I have had the opportunity to study my father's scrapbooks and diaries, along with other memorabilia, and I now realise that he did indeed accomplish a great deal during his motorcycling career, especially on his two epic trans-Canadian trips. I often think that one of those journeys could form the basis of an interesting film-perhaps the icing on the cake for his achievements.

M. Graham Oates, B.Sc, M.Sc.
Formby, Liverpool, January 2010

Graham, Graham jnr and Wynne Oates, May 1940

M. Graham Oates jnr

Acknowledgements

The author acknowledges with gratitude the assistance that he has received from the following - without their help this book could not have been written:-

Ken Ashton, Chris and Ian Corlett, Robin and Tommy Corlett, Jimmy Gibson, Ralph Hawkins, Peter Hill. Allan Johnson, Bill Lockington Marshall, Graham Oates Jnr, Bill & Gladys Penny

Amulree Publications
First published: 1993
Revised and expanded version: 2010

ISBN: 978-1-901508-13-0

Other Books by Bill Snelling

Aurora to Ariel (1st edition) - Amulree Publications (1993)
The TT in Old Photographs - Sutton Publications (1994)
The Isle of Man in Old Photographs - Sutton Publications (1995)
Keig 5 - Amulree Publications (1996)
Honda the TT Winning Years (with Peter Kneale) - Amulree Publications (1998)
History of the Manx Grand Prix (with Peter Kneale) - Amulree Publications (1998)
History of the Clubman's TT races (with Fred Pidcock) - Amulree Publications (2007)
TT and Manx Grand Prix results books - ACU & Manx Motorcycle Club (various years)

Other Books published by Amulree Publications

The Diamond King, by Brian Mylchreest (1993)
Glimpses of Old Peel, by Fred Palmer (1993)
The Velocette Saga, by C E 'Titch' Allen (1994)
Mackay Hugh Baillie Scott, by Gregory Slater (1995)
Royal Enfield, by Anne Bradford (1996)
TT Heroes, by Mike Savage (1997)
Vincents, HRDs and the IOM, by David Wright (1998)
Rough Landing or Fatal Flight, by Steve Poole (1999)
TT Mixture, by David Wright (2003)
TT Topics and Tales, by David Wright (2006)
Vincent and HRD Motorcycles, by David Wright (2005)
Travelling Marshals, by David Wright (2010)
Living to Race, Racing for a Living, by Frank Fox (2010)

Introduction

"Historians today seem to remember only the economic or political crises: perhaps the Graham Oates of the world with their idealism and optimism need to be remembered instead"

An interest in Manx motorcycling history led me to the information that ultimately resulted in this book.

I had been looking for information on both James Walter Oates, producer of the Aurora machine, and J. Graham Oates, trans-Canada pioneer. It soon became clear that these were one and the same person. I was introduced to his sister Gladys, who kindly loaned me the many scrapbooks, photo albums and diaries from which this book has been compiled.

I must heartily thank the many members of the Oates family, from here on the Isle of Man, in Liverpool and also in Canada who gave so freely of information.

My thanks also go to the Canadian Vintage Motorcycle Group, through whose efforts both I and the Canadian National Museum know much more about Canadian motor cycling than before.

I must especially single out the assistance and advice proffered by Allan Johnston of Georgetown, Ontario, not only in correcting errors and omissions on the Canadian side of the book, but also adding many fascinating insights to motorcycling of the era. The quote that heads the introduction is a line from one of Allan's letters which breathed more life into the manuscript with his observations of Canadian motorcycling in the later 20s early 30s

For reasons of continuity I have used the name Graham throughout the book, with the consent of his family.

During WWII, Graham left Wynne and son Graham, and transfered his attentions to Betty, whom he had met during his military service.

Part-way through compiling the first version of this book, I was suddenly asked by Gladys to return all the books. It appears that Betty had convinced her that my book was to 'dish the dirt' about him. I had to pen a letter to both Betty and Gladys stating that it was only my intention to chronicle the motorcycling life of J. Graham Oates, and I would not refer to his family situation. Only then was I able to complete the book.

I made contact with Graham Oates, son of J. G-O and sent him a proof copy of the book. He called when visiting the Island and asked where I had obtained the information to write the book. I pointed to the books I had collected from Gladys.

His reply was "I have never seen them!" These books, together with the bottle of water collected from the Hudson Bay in 1932, are now in his possession.

Betty never had any interest in Graham's previous life, indeed when a Canadian colleague called to see Graham at a TT, she sent him packing!

After Graham's death, Gladys called on Betty at Moose Lodge, Baldrine; she was collecting her belongings together to move to a sheltered housing complex in Ramsey.

As she walked up the garden path, she passed a dustbin, with no lid on. Glancing in she saw all Graham's books inside! "If you want them, take them now," said Betty. If that dustbin lid had been secure, all this history would have been lost!

With access to even more artifacts and photographs, I have been able to fill in gaps from the first volume.

Sadly, in the seventeen years since that volume was published, a number of the people who helped in the first book have passed on. These include: Raymond Baxter, Thomas Arthur Corlett, Jimmy Gibson, Bill Marshall, Gladys and Bill Penny.

In writing this revised book, I have been given permission by Graham Oates, Graham's son, to chronicle how the book came into being.

This was my first attempt at writing a book; for years I felt it was one that needed publishing.

I have added an extra chapter on the motoring successes of Graham's son, also Graham, author unknown.

The first version sold out; only time will tell if you feel this revised and expanded version is worth while.

I hope you find it as interesting to read as I did in researching and writing it.

Bill Snelling
Glen Road, Laxey, 2010

Chapter 1

EARLY YEARS - THE WYNNE SCOOTER AND THE AURORA

James Walter Graham Oates was born on 14th January, 1897, at 5 Hatfield Grove, Douglas, Isle of Man to John Oates, baker, and Mary (nee) Graham, housewife, the eldest of six children. He was born towards the end of the Victorian era, an age of technological discovery, a period when single horse-power transport was making way for the multi-horse-powered automobile. The Isle of Man's role as the road race capital of the world started in 1904 when Tynwald, the Island's parliament passed a far-sighted law to allow public roads to be closed for car-racing events, as the British Government would not allow the use of their roads for such follies.

From birth, Graham suffered from asthma. It was an accepted remedy at the time to return the child to where the grand parents had been brought up, but as they had also moved to the Isle of Man from their native Scotland, Graham spent some of his youth living out at the Cronk y Voddy area of the Island with his nephews. A further period of his youth was spent at a school in Nelson, Lancashire, near where his father was learning to run an insurance agency. The family eventually returned to the Island where his mother ran a boarding house at Number 5, Mona Terrace, Douglas, later moving to No. 1 in the same terrace.

The young Graham witnessed the Gordon Bennett car races, instituted in 1904, and the International motorcycle qualifying races, held in 1905 and 1906, which preceded the first TT races of 1907.

Graham obtained his first riding licence in early 1914, but did not have much time to ride on home soil. With the Great War just declared, he ran away to enlist in November of that year, but his youthfulness was discovered and he was returned to the Island. Attaining the enlistable age of 17 he once more volunteered, subsequently seeing service in the battlefields of France as a despatch rider with the 17th Lancers on both horse and motorcycle.

Commissioned and decorated in the field, he was seconded as despatch rider to the 1st Indian Cavalry for the latter part of 1915. During his first wartime period, Graham sent a number of letters to the Isle of Man Weekly Times, chronicling his wartime experiences. In one he recalled riding through a forest, when a deer ran out of the trees and bowled him off the bike,

Despatch riding on Model H Triumph
c. 1915-1916

Blackpool Hospital, 1916

injuring his left side, arm and leg, as well as killing the deer. He reported that the deer was brought in, and served up next day at the officers' mess!

It was during this period that he was caught in a gas attack, which ultimately resulted in his losing the sight of his left eye. Invalided out of the army Graham was to undergo seventeen separate operations to retain the inoperative eye, but he was doomed to monocular vision for the rest of his life.

Returning to his native Island after a long convalescence in Blackpool Hospital, Graham found the economy of the Isle of Man was in a very bad state. Tourism, one of the mainstays of the Island's finances, along with fishing, was slow to recover from the restrictions of the wartime period. Never again was the Island to see the volume of visitors that visited pre-war, which culminated in a peak figure of 29,856

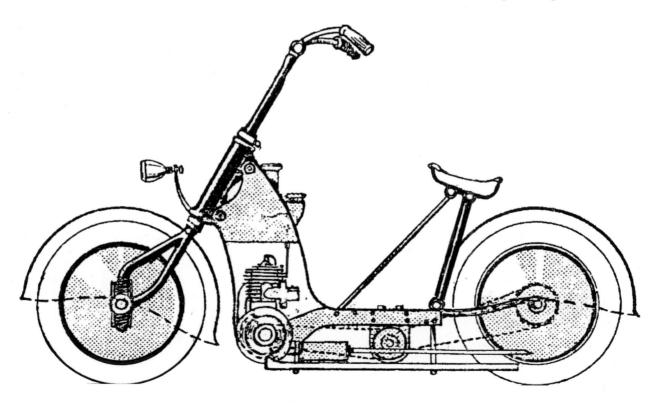

The Wynne scooter

visitors landing on the Island in a single Bank Holiday in 1913.

Graham was among many who anticipated an explosion of interest in transport after the Great War. The country's youth who returned from the war had seen at first hand the mobility that motorcycling could offer them, and they saw the advantages of being able to move quickly and freely round the country. No more were they tied to their own and neighbouring villages for work or recreation. A motorcycle was the key to their freedom.

Along with motorcycles, there was a demand for the 'scooter' type of vehicle, with small wheels and full engine enclosure. Graham produced a design for such a machine, named the Wynne, after his girlfriend, later to be his first wife. Its design was to feature a light pressed steel frame carrying an unusually large - for a scooter - 2¾ h.p. two stroke engine at its fore end, which drove a countershaft clutch; another chain transmitted the drive to the rear wheel. The machine was to be sprung fore and aft, the front by coil springs and the rear by leaf, with both wheels covered in aluminium covers, made in two halves to facilitate removal. Petrol and oil tanks were carried over the engine and at the rear the frame supported long rubber covered footboards. The whole engine was enclosed by a cover, which had convenient doors to give access to the engine etc. 16 x 3 in. wheels were to be fitted. Details and drawings of the Wynne were carried in *The Motor Cycle* of July 17th, 1919, but this machine probably only existed as a paper pipe-dream, as no one can recall Graham ever making it.

The demand for machines far outstripped supplies. The manufacturers who had supplied thousands of machines for the Allies war effort, including Triumph, Douglas, Scott, and P & M,

were working flat out in a vain effort to catch up with demand. New makers were coming into the market, ever eager to gain a slice of this lucrative market, at the rate of at least one a week in the period after the War. Some of these machines were technically innovative, - the Stanger V-twin two stroke, the Hawker, the Peters, etc. To call others 'manufacturers' is stretching a point; many of them were purely 'assemblers', gathering the required parts together from factories in the Midlands and London, building them into very ordinary machines and offering them to the public for between £27 and £100, depending on capacity, specification, etc.

Graham decided to produce his own machine and took the assembling route. Nothing was available on the Island, but it was possible to purchase all the required parts by mail order. A catalogue from Motor Services Ltd., High Holborn, London lists all the parts that were needed to build a machine. Frames suitable for various engines, the model 91 Dalm 318 cc engine, two speed Burman gearboxes, Druid forks, wheels, mudguards, tanks, rear brake assembly, levers, etc. All it needed was to manufacture the engine plates to marry all the parts, get a transfer designed and made, and you had your machine.

The first machine so produced was built in the back yard of the family home at 5, Mona Terrace, Douglas. Registered as MN 920 in the name of Wynne Brown, his girl friend, this first machine is listed with the Highway Board as a Moonbeam, possibly as an alternative to the Sunbeam, which sold well on the Island in the vintage years. Later the name Aurora was chosen for his machines which arose from an evening spent at the Picture House in Douglas. That evening he saw a film of the Aurora

Graham and John Oates, Snaefell Summit, Good Friday, 1919

Borealis, the Northern Lights. (The Aurora name had been used in 1902 for a machine made in Coventry, but there was no connection between these two machines).

Not long after assembling the first machine, and with it in an unpainted state, Graham made his first climb to the summit of Snaefell on Good Friday, 1919. Judging from the photo taken at the time, with his father in attendance, and noting the cushion strapped to the rear carrier, I would imagine that Oates Snr. was carried up the Mountain in this fashion, at least as far as the Bungalow Hotel, from where Graham made a successful straight-up climb to the top. A much easier route would have been to trace the Snaefell Mountain Railway that winds its way to the 2036 ft. summit.

In later life J.W. Graham Oates was to become a legend for his exploits on the rail tracks that he bypassed that Good Friday morning.

Three days after that inaugural ascent Graham rode the machine in the Wallace Shield Trial, an annual Easter Monday run-around event which started and finished in Douglas. It was not an auspicious start, as the Dalm engine was not as sprightly as hoped. Niggling little problems like the HT lead coming adrift stopped him a few times, and he finished well down the field. Despite this, he was determined to prove the machines capabilities, and announced in the local press that he was to enter it in the 1920 TT races.

Up to this point Graham had funded the project with his savings and demob gratuity. His father John, who operated the Britannic Insurance agency from an office in Well Road Hill, Douglas, provided financial aid, but a further injection of capital was required to put the Aurora company on a firm footing.

Graham had befriended George Parsons Crellin, another WW1 survivor, who was one of four brothers from a farming family at Ballachurry, St. Judes. Like all his brothers,

George was mad keen on bikes. When Graham approached him with the offer of a partnership in the Aurora project, he was instantly agreeable, putting up £100, a mighty sum of money in those days. Reservations were voiced about the project by many of his friends and family, but Graham won George's commitment with his enthusiasm for the machine.

With the finances secure, the Queen's Hall in Ramsey was rented, and a workforce assembled to build the machines. Work on producing the bikes was slow, and Graham's father, intent on seeing what was becoming of his investment, often complained to his daughter Gladys that more often than not he found the workforce playing tennis on the adjacent courts instead of building bikes. The initial workforce comprised

Jack Oates on the 4¼ h.p. Blackburne Aurora, outside the Queen's Hall, Ramsey where they were built

Graham and the first Dalm-powered Aurora, outside the Isle of Man Bank, Athol Street, Douglas

Bill Buckley and Fred Wilson.

The first Ramsey-built machine was completed and sold to a customer in Scotland, then they set about building and preparing a pair of machines for the 1920 Junior TT, the first to be held after the Great War. It was the first to use the full Mountain Course as we know it today, adding the Cronk ny Mona, Signpost Corner and Governors Bridge section to take the course to its length of 37.73 miles.

Graham was entered as No. 26, with the second Aurora at No. 18, ridden by Norman C. Sclater Jnr, an amateur rider from Liverpool who rode a Norton 16H in reliability trials. It could possibly have been the same machine that he had entered in the 1920 Senior TT, as in the

early days the only distinction between a trials and a racing machine was in the choice of tyres!

For the Aurora two Dalm 318 cc two stroke engines, (73 x 76 bore/stroke), were 'tuned to the best of their ability', to quote Graham's words, by their makers, J.C. Dalman & Sons, River Street, Birmingham. For the race, a Birmingham built Juckes four-speed gearbox was installed in place of the two speed Burman unit.

The Aurora has been erroneously described in reference books as having a double acting rear brake, with a brake shoe pressing on both the inside and the outside of the belt rim. Nothing so elaborate was used on the Aurora, but this feature was to be found on the innovative

Peters, a machine that was marketed from Parliament Street, Ramsey, but was never in fact built on the Island.

Considering it was a machine manufactured on the Island, it took a long time for the Aurora to venture forth in TT practice. A newspaper report written halfway through practice week quoted "Local rider Oates and his Aurora have not yet been seen in practice, but the machine has been often heard in the vicinity of Mount Havelock" adjacent to his Mona Terrace home.

When he finally started practice, it was obvious from the outset that the machine was not in race trim. The Juckes box gave no end of trouble, and Graham later commented that he used to find more neutrals than gears. His first practice lap lasted only as far as Quarter Bridge before the footrests folded up, and subsequent laps proved that he had no chance of getting in a qualifying lap under seventy minutes, which was under 35 mile an hour average. He managed to complete only three laps in a full week of practising, with his best time being ninety five minutes fifty seconds. He was never able to string two laps together, as so many parts had fallen off the bike on the first circuit to prohibit him trying for two on the trot. "How really he is going to qualify is a mystery" was another comment from a local paper.

In addition to the bike's shortcomings, the state of the TT circuit did not help. It was in an appalling condition, as no repairs had been

Tommy Corlett took this picture in 1920, outside the Queens Hall, Ramsey. 'In charge' is George Crellin, the middleman is Graham's brother Jack Oates, with Graham on the carrier. The machine is George's 4¼ h.p. Blackburn engined Aurora.

carried out since long before wartime. The stretch of road from Sulby through to Ramsey was either dusty or one long mud bath, dependent on the weather. The Mountain Road was no better than two dusty cart tracks and it took great nerve to switch ruts to pass a slower competitor when traversing this part of the course. Even when maintenance took place it was of no great help, as fork jarring potholes would be transformed into mini pyramids the next time the riders came round. Meeting a road repairing steam roller round a bend was another hazard frequently encountered that year! Tarmac was not laid on any Island road until 1922, when a stretch - 'for experimental purpose' - to quote a Highway Board note, was laid from Quarter Bridge to Braddan Bridge. Up until 1927 the practices were held on open roads, and the riders had not only to contend with the Mountain course's myriad bends, but

had to dodge all the other wheeled traffic, or pedestrian road users. It took the unfortunate death of Archie Birkin in a collision with a fish cart that year to persuade the authorities to close the roads for practice as well as the races.

Contemporary practice reports observed that the Aurora may not have been the fastest machine around, but it certainly was the noisiest! It is easy with hindsight to suggest that a piston ported two-stroke would have run far more efficiently with its silencer fitted instead of running with two very short exhaust pipes. Sclater does not appear in any practice reports with the machine, which suggests that only a single Aurora was readied for the race.

With Graham unable to meet the qualifying time, Norman Sclater was given the honour of riding the Aurora in the Junior TT, having qualified easily on his Senior Norton. *The Motor Cycle* claimed that "N. C. Sclater

Norman Sclater with his Senior TT Norton

(Aurora) roared away', but his progress was not in keeping with that meteoric start. After faltering for several miles the Aurora finally packed up just past Hillberry with a broken compression release valve, causing the machine to briefly catch fire at Cronk ny Mona. So the only Manx built motorcycle was destined not to complete a lap on its home course. Sclater was more fortunate in the Senior race, finishing fourth on his Norton.

After this poor showing interest in the Aurora declined, despite the public being exhorted in an advertisement to "join our waiting list now to ensure immediate delivery"! Only two 3 hp machines were registered on the Island, the aforementioned 'Moonbeam' - MN 920, and MN 1063, registered on 19th May, 1920. It appears that only one further Aurora was built. This was fitted with a 4¼ hp (550cc) side-valve Blackburne engine and was built for George Crellin, co-founder of the firm, and registered MN 1246 on 13th September 1920.

By this time, Graham had become disillusioned with the whole business, as financial problems were causing a rift between the partners. The firm owed rent and rates on the Queen's Hall, and sales, never good, had dwindled to zero. Graham was to comment in later life that it had been a "conceited idea" to manufacture bikes with such limited knowledge at his disposal. But, if the TT venture had gone better for the firm, it might have been possible to attract more backing.

Youthful enthusiasm had overcome financial caution, a common enough occurrence, even in today's high finance world.

Word reached George Crellin that the Coroner was on his way to seize the firm's assets, possibly due to non payment of the rent. Wishing to retain something from his investment he set to and shipped everything out of the Queen's Hall factory by hand cart, depositing it in Kewley's cycle shop, half a mile away. When the Coroner arrived, the only 'assets' he seized were a broken chain and a burst inner tube! George Crellin was able to sell enough of the firm's hardware to get back part of his outlay, but two machines, including the racer, were left in a derelict shed for many years, until George Young, the local scrap dealer, put them in a scrap boat bound for Barrow.

George Crellin, although somewhat embittered by the lack of success for the Aurora project, later provided capital to start Ramsey Motors, which was to became Island Garages, one of the Island's largest motor traders.

The only surviving Aurora artifact is a petrol tank that George Young gave to Tommy Corlett as he was loading the bikes onto the scrap ship, as a souvenir of his first job. This tank is now exhibited at the ARE motorcycle museum in Kirk Michael.

Thomas Arthur Corlett joined the firm late in 1920, just before it closed down. Tommy was paid 10/- a week for his first job. It was Tommy's father who tipped Crellin off about the coroner's imminent arrival, and George had admired Tommy's mechanical skill in maintaining his father's Eadie quadricycle, one of the first vehicles registered on the Island as MN 22.

George Crellin used his Aurora-Blackburne for a number of years, both as daily transport, and in the many speed trials held all over the Island. He later sold it to purchase a more sporty machine, a Norton BRS - Brookiands Racing Special. The new owner of the Aurora-Blackburne, who lived at Kerrowmooar, arrived at Tommy's home one day with the gearbox making a horrendous, shrieking noise. "Better put some oil in that" said Tommy. "But I put half a pint of oil in it yesterday," said the owner. 'Paraffin oil"! A quick drain and refill with a more suitable lubricant, and he went away delighted that Tommy Corlett had somehow effected a magical cure.

But by the time Tommy joined the firm, Graham had severed all links and was already making plans to move across the water.

A group of Sunday riders, snapped on Ramsey Promenade. Left to right: Thomas Arthur Corlett Snr (Ivy Vitesse), Thomas Arthur Corlett Jnr (baby Triumph) and George Parsons Crellin (Aurora-Blackburne)

Chapter 2
IN THE TRADE, TRIALS AND THE 1924 ULTRA LIGHTWEIGHT TT

Not long after the 1920 TT and the events described in the previous chapter, Graham moved across the Irish Sea to Birmingham, where his initial job was working for Dunlop as a tyre tester. Whilst there he made friends with the Burman brothers, Harry and Jim, who were at that time making a good living out of making small farm implements, horse clippers and turnip cutters. They were also making a very basic 2 speed gearbox for the many lightweight proprietary engined machines on the burgeoning bike market. Harry was keen to expand the gearbox side of the firm, but Jim was happy to carry on making the shears and cutters. With the assistance of Briggs, their gearbox designer, and the encouragement of Graham, designs for a 3-speed box with clutch were drawn up. The Burman boys were keen for Graham to work for them, but he declined the offer until they had the gearbox built and ready for testing, when he left Dunlop's employment and moved to the Ryland Road gearbox manufacturers.

The prototype gearbox was fitted into a Blackburne engined Marloe. This very basic Bordesley-built machine was then taken by Graham into the Malvern Hills to see if the box would stand up to the task. The gearbox stood the test no problem, but the Marloe kept breaking its frame around the steering head, dropping the motor down on its outside flywheel. Twice he had to call out the Marloe mechanic to go to Malvern and re-frame the machine before Harry Burman told him to

'bring the bloody thing back before you bust it again!'.

In addition to being the chief tester for the Burman gearboxes, he was acting, unpaid, as their salesman-cum-promotions executive. By this fashion Graham got to know many manufacturers, some well established, others in the throes of joining the still expanding market. He heard of a new firm who might be potential candidates for the gearbox, and called on them in Delbarn Road, Birmingham. It would be fair to say that his arrival at Massey Arran was somewhat premature for when he first set eyes on their bike, it was merely a full scale chalk drawing on the specially sanded office floor!

The Burman brothers and Graham gave the designers Mr. Massey and Mr. Vaughan as much assistance as they could to complete the machines. With a country wide coal strike looking like it would stop Massey Arran getting their first bikes built, Burman, with their own power generating plant, made the hubs, sprockets, etc. Engine plates were cut from turnip cutters, plenty strong enough, and Graham was their test pilot when the first machine was made. The first Burman 3-speed gearbox was fitted to the prototype Massey Arran, but the metal machine did not at first live up to its chalked promise, and a rapid frame redesign was called for at this early stage. An early model was taken down to Brooklands by C.M. Fairweather who was to ride a Blackburne in the TT. It was not long before reports came back that the steering was still not up to scratch and another redesign was called for. Finally, a suitable frame was designed and Massey Arran declared their intention to enter three machines for the 1921 Junior TT.

The Massey Arran entries showed the variety of power plants that were available at that time to the multitude of small manufacturers. One was side-valve JAP powered, to be ridden by Jack Thomas, the second used the side-valve Blackburne power unit and was to be ridden by Jack Holroyd. Their third entry was to be powered by the new, very competitive ohv outside-flywheel Blackburne unit. This latter bike was to be ridden by J. Graham Oates, so little wonder he was so keen to help them succeed with the project.

The team arrived on the Island midway through the practice period and set up camp at the Creg Malin Hotel on Peel Promenade, along with the Levis and Martin teams. As soon as the team arrived, Graham was approached by A. G. Miller, one of the Martin riders who was keen to try the new Burman 3-speed gearbox in the machine of his own manufacture. Even as late as halfway through the practice period some firms were still experimenting to get the right set-up for their machines!

Graham's first practice lap that year was also to be his last. In common with all teams based at Peel, he started this lap from Ballacraine, a normal practice in those early days with race team headquarters spread all round the Island. This meant he had to ride three quarters of a lap before he got to the Grandstand to be timed. On this first lap the Massey was really flying, much faster than last year's Aurora. He easily caught, passed and left Eric Williams, winner of the 1914 Junior on his AJS. But enthusiasm got the better of Graham and, attempting to take Hillberry far too fast, he hit the steps to Hillberry House and fell off. He later blamed faulty fitting of his Hutchinson tyres, but an eye witness claimed that he came down at one a hell of a lick, and simply failed to get round.

So Massey Arran were left not only with an injured rider, but the accident had wrecked the motor of their number one machine. Undaunted, Massey enlisted the services of a young amateur rider, James Whalley, a prominent trials rider in the North, and Senior TT entrant on a Sunbeam. Another ohv Blackburne motor was built from spares, the cycle parts were straightened, and on this hastily repaired machine young Whalley took on the might of the all-conquering AJS team.

Third on the first lap, he progressed to take the lead at the end of the third lap, then fell back to second place on the penultimate lap behind Eric Williams (AJS). The last lap failed to bring a nail-biting finish. Rounding Windy Corner the rear tyre went flat, Whalley took to the grass and fell off, tearing the exhaust pipe from the head and ripping the rear tyre from the rim. Remounting unhurt save a bloody nose, and stuck in

Jack Holroyd (Massey Arran)

2nd gear, he made the finish in 5th place, first non AJS home, a tremendous debut for a machine that only months previously had just been a chalk drawing on an office floor.

Still working for Burman's, Graham had taken to riding the one day sporting and long distance trials that were held most weekends all over England, Wales and Scotland. He rode a variety of makes of machines in these trials, each different, but with one common factor, they were all equipped with the Burman gearbox.

For the ACU Six Day Trial of 1921, Graham was mounted on a Blackburne engined Edmund. This Chester-built machine was fitted with an early form of cantilever sprung frame, which had received much praise in the motorcycling press, and it was making its competition debut on the event.

The 1921 730 mile event started and finished at Brooklands and took in all the major hills in Southern England. This was to be one of the easiest events in the history of the trial. 54 out of the 68 finishers claimed gold medals, five silver medals were won, three bronze and 5 riders claimed certificates for finishing the event outside of medal standard. Amongst those to claim only a certificate was Graham. On the very first special test, a brake efficiency test down the Test Hill in Brooklands, the rear brake cable snapped and Graham inadvertently made one of the fastest times of the day down the Hill! This lost him the maximum 25 marks for the test and he was to lose further marks throughout the trial. His luck was out right to the end of the trial, and he was to suffer the

Graham with his 1921 trials Edmund

The Edmund team at their TT headquarters, 1922. It is captioned 'At our depot'. Right to left are Geo W. Shepherd, rider (8th in Junior); George Edward (Ted) Partin, Company Secretary; Graham Oates "tester on our staff, wanted to ride but only had one eye"; Gerald Brown, rider (retired, Junior); remaining two believed to be on staff of 'The Motor Cycle'

Graham displays a 1922 production model 4B Edmund. This was fitted with a 349cc Blackburne sv engine and 3-speed Burman gearbox, with hub brakes fore and aft and a saddle tank

The Grindley JAP that finally succumbed to valve trouble in the 1922 ACU Six Days Trial

indignity of having to ride the final speed test at Brooklands in company with the sidecars and cyclecars, having overslept on the Saturday morning, missing his allotted starting time for his class.

Graham fared no better in the 1922 ACU Six Day Trial. Riding a 250 cc Grindley Peerless, the JAP engine repeatedly suffered from broken valves all through the event, and when yet another valve failed during the final speed test, held once again at Brooklands, he was unable to get the valve cap off to replace it. He blamed his starting number 13 - for all his troubles in this trial. He continued to ride trials with a reasonable amount of success, mixed with the occasional outing at Brooklands, but in common with all Manxmen with motorcycling in their blood, he still hankered for a successful

TT ride. The chance came with his involvement in the Powell firm in 1924. He was campaigning their machine in trials alongside T. G. 'Tommy' Meeten, when news came through that the Auto Cycle Union had been persuaded to put on an Ultra Lightweight TT race for machines of up to 175 cc.

Manufacturers of lightweights could see the kudos gained by the makers of their larger counterparts, so they asserted that a similar race for their machines would prove the stamina and reliability of their smaller engined machines to the general public. A 170 cc machine was listed in the Powell range, so it was not long before Graham had implanted the idea of running a pair of machines on the Island. The Wrexham firm entered both Graham and Arthur Greenwood. The Powell range had received

Typical scenes from the ACU Six Days Trials of the 1920s

much praise in the technical press for its handling qualities, with its steeply raked top tube that finished at about crankcase height with the Villiers motor steeply inclined, a feature of all Powells.

Seventeen starters faced the flag for this, the first ever massed start race on the Isle of Man Mountain Course. Graham recalled his experiences in the race in an article written in 1958 entitled 'My last race - The first "Ultra-Lightweight" - 1924'.

What, write a story of the 1924 T.T.? A difficult request, I find it almost impossible to remember what happened last year, let alone 34 years ago, when motorcycles had small section tyres, push-bike brakes - or little better - no steering dampers and certainly no rear springing - unless the rider had a well-padded behind to absorb the shocks, of which the Island course has many.

Some of the machines were good, some not so good; some steered, but most of them lacked precise navigation, especially on the rough parts of the course. The Sulby stretch, after rain, caused much blasphemy, and the section from Quarry Bends, as they are now known, to Ramsey was just mud and ruts - and it was little better when dry, owing to the dust. Certainly all this was living in the past.

The lovely wee Island in June 1924 - and thanks to the gods it was fine for the 175 cc Ultra Lightweight race and the first massed

The very first massed start TT. The 1924 Ultra Lightweight gets under way. Graham is No. 8. The front row lineup is: No. 1 Jock Porter (New Gerrard) the winner, Geoff Davison (Levis) 4th and Alec Bennett (Diamond) 9th

start to be seen on the TT circuit. Some 20 odd riders were on the grid waiting for the maroon which would send them on their way and confound the many critics who predicted a pile-up at Quarter Bridge. I have wondered whose elbow would be in my ribs and whose footrest would be cuddling the spokes of my front wheel - but fears were foundless.

My starting number was eight and strange to say I finished in eighth position - to put the end of my story to the beginning...

Looking back at photographs one sees various makes of machines that have long since ceased to be made. Mostly two-strokes are in favour with the exception of those fitted with the special ohv Blackburne engines - and they were more or less standard with raised compression ratios and mostly using 'dope'- P.M.S. 1. (fuel).

If the Blackburnes keep going - and they have a disconcerting habit of throwing away their push-rods when you most wanted them not to - the winner will be found from Wal Handley (Rex Acme), Jock Porter (New Gerrard), Freddie Morgan (Cotton) and local boy Chris Stead, also on a Cotton, but Geoff Davison on his light and speedy two-stroke Levis will be up in front.

Can't resist a smile when I think of Ultra Lightweights! My Powell scaled 258 lbs. Down hill it went quite well, but it could not be considered fast and it suffered, as did many two-strokes, with such vibration that it could not be driven on full throttle over the downhill section from Kate's Cottage to Hillberry. It would eight-stroke, four-stroke and do all the other strokes but it wouldn't two-stroke! After one lap my hands, arms, neck and head felt numbed, and I many times wondered that the handlebars did not snap.

The way the wee Powell could be cornered on its footrests though, was a delight, and I well remember the present High Bailiff, then a marshal at Ballacraine, saying, "That bike will slip from under you if you're not careful, so keep it upright - at least until you're out of my section!"

Waiting on the grid, looking around and hoping that you aren't obviously suffering with fright... Will it start - always a worry - and if so where and when would it stop? That is, if it starts without galloping a mile and changing a plug. Cold engine starts in those days.

An anxious glance at your pit - and they certainly were different from those of today. You filled up from a petrol tin and plunged the tang end of a file into the bottom to give a quicker flow, and filler caps were usually of the screw-on variety. What's a handful of minutes between friends?

The riders were dressed in an odd assortment of kit - not as today in space suits. Some had grey flannels tucked into their boots; woollen sweaters were very popular and although crash helmets were the drill, I have often wondered if they all passed the ACU's test. Was it Reuben Harveyson who wore a bowler hat in practice?

My own kit? Leather waistcoat, riding breeches - legacy of the '14-18 war - golf hose, suede shoes held on with Mr. Dunlop's or Mr. Hutchinson's rubber bands. Most useful to hold the bike together too, if necessary - that is, if the very generous lashing of insulating tape should give trouble.

Ready for the off, but not by any means sure that my bike would even reach Ballacraine. Unfortunately I had burst a piston on the last lap of practice, and had taken a spare out of my trials machine. And to make matters worse, during an unofficial run on the mountain part of the course, the late Billy Hollowell passed me

Ramsey Hairpin on the Powell

and a stone from the rear wheel of his Norton broke my one and only pair of glasses, fortunately without eye damage.

That entailed a hasty trip to a Douglas optician who promised speedy replacement. Race morning on the way to the start, and panic - shop closed! Left one of Powell chaps to find specs' mender, grab the glasses and taxi in haste to the start.

Minutes ticked away, anxious glances to the pit area, but no glasses...

The maroon fires and we are off I like a blind man, worried as much for others as myself. Quarter Bridge - all bunched together, with the exception of the Blackburnes and the Levises who are well ahead. Can remember rubbing elbows with, amongst others, Alec Bennett, Douglas Prentice, Norman Black, Gus Kuhn,

Arthur Greenwood and a couple of Wee McGregor riders.

Soon I am well in the rear and by the time Ramsey is in sight must surely be the last on the road. Up the mountain I feel the need of a pair of pedals - and stouter legs than mine to push them - but we are still going, which is something. Past the Bungalow and on to Kate's Cottage - the engine is certainly improving.

Down the mountain - don't two strokes make a fuss on full throttle downhill! Careful around Governors and on to the Grandstand; a glance at the clock and methinks I'll need lights before the end of the race; a wave from my pit attendant who hadn't expected me to do a lap any more than I had.

On the second lap the wee bike either got faster or my blind navigation was improving, *for I actually began to overhaul someone! Slowly but surely I passed Alec Bennett - but no one ever overtook Alec unless his machine was sick, so there was no inward cheering on my part.*

Approaching Ramsey I tripped over a cat yes, a black one, not Manx, who chose the moment of my passing to cross the road. Don't know the fate of the cat, but when I put the front brake on in Ramsey the lever came up to the handlebar. No brake - the rod had pulled away from the nipple. Nothing much to worry about, only need brakes at about half a dozen places, at the speeds of those days...

Back to the pits for a replenishment and ask "Where is everyone?" for apart from the few between the start and Ballacraine, first lap and then, Alec Bennett, I had been having a solitary ride. "here's your glasses, just keep going" were the instructions bawled into my ear - just as well my attendant shouted, for I was almost deaf.

This encouragement put new life into me - ye gods, I can actually see my way down Bray Hill without guessing where the road should be! Vibration or not, go on you little devil - and now at last we will be able to see the corners not to mention the ruts, grass and stones on the Mountain.

So the last lap was the fastest - at almost 41 mph. Sounds silly to mention such a speed in these days of 100 mph laps, but things were different then. The wee Powell put up a stout show with its sick engine and a half blind jockey. As I said in the first part of the story, it came in eighth and was actually the third two stroke to finish. Not so bad after all.

Team mate Arthur Greenwood was destined to retire his Powell in this race, to join the other five rides - five retirements that he clocked up in his abortive TT career.

The Villiers motor was certainly no match for the Blackburne four stroke power unit of the race winning New Gerrard, but no matter, for it gave him his cherished ambition of competing in and finishing in a TT race. This was to be his last attempt at TT racing, and indeed his last motorcycling foray for the next four years.

Chapter 3

BOLIVIA - CANADA - THE FIRST TRANS-CANADA TRIP

Around the time of the '24 TT, Graham was advised to move abroad to a warmer climate for the sake of his health, as the injuries he sustained in the First War were troubling him. He set himself Australia as the target and mentioned his emigration plans to Count Delgado, a Brooklands car racer. The Count had interests in the Guggenheim tin mining prospects in the Andes, and was on the lookout for a trustworthy person to go out to Bolivia and run the engineering works at a new mining site they were just about to start work on. The salary Delgado offered Graham was so tempting that in under three weeks from the end of the 1924 TT, he had left Burman's employment to set sail for South America and the Guggenheim mine.

Graham landed at Antofagasta, the Chilean town used mainly as the outgoing seaport for Bolivian ore. From this port he travelled for three days

One horse power - Andes, South America

into the interior to Potosi, Bolivia's second city, the highest city in the world. Here he was met by a courier for the firm with two pack mules. This was the only method of transport to the mine site at that time, set high in the Andes, 14,000 ft. above sea level and 1,400 miles distant from the Pacific coast. Every single piece of equipment had to be transported by either pack mule or pack llama, as pack horses could not work in the rarefied atmosphere. He was intrigued to witness the mule and llama train winding its way along a narrow track on the side of a mountain, - the narrowness of these trails prohibiting any other means of transport. It was only later in his time at the mine that transportation facilities vastly improved, which assisted in the expansion of exports to all regions of the world. His work at the Potosi Mine consisted chiefly of overseeing constructional work, road making, and repairing motors. He was instrumental in bringing to the site, and constructing, the first tin dredge in the Andes, every part of which had to be transported in by mules and assembled on the spot. It took eight months to bring this particular piece of machinery in, and all the drudgery was done by native labour. The first motor lorry to go into the district was taken in by Graham, but it required the help of 200 men to blast, quarry, and dig the roads it used, and they literally had to carry it through some of the passes. His lack of any knowledge of the local language did not make any difference, but he soon learnt one word in the local dialect, it meant "push"!

During his time in Bolivia, Graham spent some time writing articles about the country, the mines, and the Indians, many of which appeared in American and Canadian newspapers.

In one of Graham's unpublished articles he relates a hair-raising adventure at the mill when he went to visit the mine workings. It is entitled 'An Engineer in South America'.

It is not readily understood what privations, risks and struggles men take, and what dangers that are braved to obtain the mineral which is commonly known as tin. But it is my endeavour here to relate in my small way, but one of the many instances of risks taken in the extraction of that widely used mineral from the high Andes of Bolivia. An aerial railway is used to carry the tin bearing earth from the mines down to the

The tin dredge - Carracoles Mine, Bolivia

A general view of the Carracole Mine, Bolivia, showing the aerial bucket line

mill, there to pass through its many processes on its way to supply the ever hungry market for this metal. I have decided that today I will make the trip to the mines, which are located in the adjoining mountains some six miles away, in one of the steel cages which are used for carrying the ore. These run up and down on steel cables, and pass over towers every half mile or so apart and about one hundred feet high, the height, of course, depending on the nature of the ground to be passed over. The strength and reliability of the cables is a constant source of wonderment, and it is a rare occasion that an accident occurs, beyond the fracturing of the cable where it enters the drum of the winch. This part of the

description of the cables and the accidents that occur to them has a considerable bearing on the latter part of my story. I glance at my watch which points to the hour of eight, and with a cheery wave of my hand I curl myself up in the cage, which will, for the next hour, be my sole support between life and death. It will take a considerable stretch of the imagination to call this little steel house either comfortable or clean, but it means a considerable saving of time going via the bucket line, in preference to the mule train.

...I am now moving at a steady speed of about four miles an hour, up the steep climb of the mountainside, the cage riding very steadily and

with but little noise, higher and higher, now passing over huge rocks below me, and the next few yards still bearing their streams of ice from the freezing of the night. This ice has not as yet come under the strong sunlight to allow of it thawing, and again, for the day, becoming a pretty little stream of fresh cool water, to gladden the heart of the animals that live in the lands far below. On turning a point in the aerial route we swing around a high precipice and then a glorious sight is revealed: the mountains all capped with snow as far the vision reaches. Cold and stark they extend skywards, here and there the tops are enshrouded with the morning mist, which is being wafted on majestically by the scarcely perceptible breeze...

Out over the glacial lake the cage sails like a passing cloud, and it produces a sense of awe to watch the shadows changing, the sun glistening and reflecting on the placid, transparent waters far below. My mind momentarily goes back to counting the number of buckets that to my knowledge have found watery billets in the depths of these innocent waters. I shudder to think of the fate of any human being, should they be unfortunate enough to drop from this 900 ft. height into the ice cold water below...

My reflections are however short-lived, and with a thumping clanking noise I hear the steel cable going over the pulley wheels in the next tower. This I know to be the last before I sail off over the gulch of the famed Santa Rosa open span. This marks the take off of the highest aerial bucket line in the world. With a bump and a lurch we are over the tower and mildly swinging and rocking out over space. Higher and higher still we climb, the ground receding rapidly behind us. The valley below merges into the hillside, and the small glaciers seem to link their way down through the terrific

mountainside, holding it seemingly together by their ice cold and silver threads here and there, winding in and out. I notice thin yellow threads which from experience I know to be trails, used for countless years by the Indian llama and mule herders for the transportation of the supplies. Taking my eyes from the ground below, I glimpse two of the feathered denizens of the Andes. Out over the centre of the valley, 18,000 ft. above sea level, and I am feeling slight effects of the terrific height...

A jerk! Heavens, what has happened? Have winch operators gone mad? Do they not know that a man is suspended out over this gulch in a crazy bucket, not large enough for a dog kennel? Nothing but a cable between life and death! Thank God, I am moving again, slowly it's true. With a drop which almost sickens me, the bucket falls and swings down through space. The cable sags, drops, and in a state of fear I grip it with my hands in an effort of sheer desperation. I have been in some strange predicaments in my life and have usually escaped with but little injury, but this is evidently the end. Down ten, twenty, thirty feet or more, it feels like hundreds and time seems eternity. I still clutch the cable with frozen hands, and pray that all will still be well. What is happening? Has the cable broken and is now dragging itself slowly over the mountainside by the combined weight of the swinging bucket and cable? Life is mocking me as I hang in space over this terrible chasm...

..But surely my eyes deceive me! Is that not the cable moving away on the other side ahead of me. Yes, yes, it is on the upwards sway, and the mistake or trouble must have been rectified. I feel like cheering, so glad is my heart. I had only expected death in a ghastly manner on the rocks of the gorge below. But I am thankful to *see the cable becoming tighter with each revolution of the faraway winch. What has been the most trying time of my life is now passing, and the torture which seems to have gone on for hours is almost ended. It was not for some days afterwards that the reason of my unfortunate experience was explained to me. The winchman, working the cable winches at the mining end, noticed a slight break in the cable, where it enters the drum. He immediately stopped the winch and allowed the cable to run backward. He then clamped another piece of spare cable to the existing one below the break, after which the broken part was cut off and entered into the winch. Then he hauled up the slack and unhooked the spare cable, after which he ran the machinery in the usual manner. Fate decreed that I, unknown to the operators, was to be the poor unfortunate being to have the experience of being suspended over space deprived of the power of informing anyone of my terrible plight.*

Although he did not see a motorcycle and rarely a car, during the years he spent at the Carracoles mine, as his transport at the mine was of the single horse power variety, powered transport was never far from his thoughts.

Another of the many articles he wrote during his time at the mine is entitled 'Across the Three American Continents by Motor'. American President Collidge had remarked that he foresaw the day ahead when it would be possible to journey by road from New York to Buenos Aires. The idea of such a journey made quite an impression on Graham. The many hours he spent considering all aspects of such a trip must have been a mentally stimulating 'escape vehicle' from his self imposed exile in the high altitude world of mountains, mines, and Indians.

The itinerary of Graham's 'trip' was to be New York, Buffalo, Philadelphia, Cleveland, Detroit, Chicago, Omaha, Denver, San Francisco and Los Angeles. Down through Mexico which was then in quite an unsettled state, passing Mexico City and on through the State of Guatemala to Central America via Costa Rica. Through the Panama Zone, Panama City, Colon, Bogota, Lima, Le Paz and Potosi (where this was being written). Onwards to the wilds of North Western Argentina ending in Buenos Aires, the journey to have taken about 8 months. Graham writes:-

"At the outset it is made clear that full use will be made of cooperation with various motor agents, in conjunction with radio broadcasting stations to arrange interviews and photo sessions in the towns they pass. When passing through Bolivia he suggests the use of the side track of the railway, 'We again start to climb the winding railway line up in to the Andes". The final paragraph of this article gives a significant clue to his pursuit of such a trip, one that he was to make within a year. It reads:-

"My conclusions are that the journey across the three American States is possible, and the first persons who accomplish it, will go down in to the annals as a most wonderful trip, a glorious story of adventure, and will give publicity to the interested parties which would be difficult to value in actual figures from a financial point of view."

The seed of an idea was sown, and it was to grow to fruition through a chance meeting thousands of miles away.

By the Autumn of 1927, Graham was tiring of his job at the mine and was longing to get away. The abject loneliness of being the only foreigner on site all year was one reason, but another was the antics of the Indian work force, which would stage a revolt at the drop of a hat, and two on Sundays when they had more time! They were also addicted to chewing the leaves of the coca plant, cocaine in the raw, which could explain some of their actions. Its invigorating effect must have helped them through the long hours they worked and also at the great altitude where they were working. Indeed the Bolivian Government, knowing the habits of its Indian population, passed a law which had to be strictly adhered to by all employers of native labour. It made the ruling that all native workers should be given at least forty minutes in each working day for the consumption of coca, - in effect, a narcosis tea break!

On September 2, 1927 Graham sailed from Valparaiso on the Grace Line steamer Santa Elisa, - bound for New York. It was his intention to return to the Isle of Man for a period then return to settle in Canada. Any thoughts of returning to that Bolivian mine were firmly set to the back of his mind! After a month's duck shooting in Nebraska, curtailed when someone blasted the bottom out of the canoe, he travelled north to Canada, intending to sail for England and then return to his native Isle of Man.

The day after landing in Toronto, he was walking up Danforth Avenue when he espied a motorcycle shop, the first he had seen for three years. Those years must have seemed like a lifetime for such an avid motorcycle enthusiast as Graham. This was the head branch of J.V. & J.W. Conroy, 'Dominion Distributors of Ariel, Douglas and Royal Enfield'. He stood for many minutes looking through the window at their

The Conroy Store, 516 Danforth Avenue, Toronto

selection, when he became aware of a salesman hovering close by. This young man inquired if he was interested in the bikes. Graham was, he confessed, but not in the manner that would bring about a sale or commission for the salesman, as he was shortly bound for the shores from whence Conroy's stock had arrived.

Later that same day, decked out in borrowed riding gear and astride an Ariel 500 loaned by his new found friend, Graham went for his first ride in Canada, a 100 mile (160 km) run to Hamilton and back. Returning the gear and bike with great reluctance, he spent the next few hours talking bikes before returning to his hotel. The next morning a message was sent asking him to call back at the shop. Guessing that the young salesman still had not given up hope of a sale, he returned to the showroom.

Just after Graham left the shop the previous evening, the Castrol Oil representative arrived. Charles Dennis Browne, a nephew of Lord Wakefield had been sent out from England to sell Castrol lubricants in Canada. The salesman had spoken of the Manxman who called earlier that day and Browne recognised the description as his wartime colleague Graham Oates, who was in the Cavalry when Browne was a subaltern in the Royal Horse Artillery during WW 1. This called for a party - not that either of them needed any excuse!

During that gloriously boozy evening Dennis confided that sales of Castrol oil was virtually nil in the past two years, as they faced stiff competition from the local lubricants. What was needed, suggested Graham, was a publicity stunt to bring the name of Castrol to the attention of the motoring public in Canada. The whisky flowed, ideas flowed, and by the next morning the bare bones of an idea that was

hatched in the High Andes were being fleshed out. Graham was to ride a British motorcycle and sidecar lubricated with Castrol Oil from the East - Atlantic coast to the West - Pacific coast, staying on Canadian soil all the way. There had been many attempts by car to conquer the trans-Canada route, but Graham's reasoning behind trying it with an outfit was the small size and bulk could be rescued far more easily than a car.

Roads of varying qualities were available for a large part of the trip, but there was a stretch of 900 miles between Sault Ste. Marie, Ontario and Whitemouth, Manitoba where the only link was the rail tracks. This railroad mileage passes through mile after mile of dense forest or clings to cliffs along the wild shore of Lake Superior. Parts are built over incredible swamps and bogs. In the 1880s when it was being built, as many as six tracks were laid in some places, one on top of another, since a track laid one day on apparent solid ground had sunk out of sight by the next morning. A road was not completed across this part of Canada until World War II. Until the Canadian Pacific and other railways finally tunnelled, bridged, or blasted their way through the mountains in 1926, Canada was almost two separate countries with a common parliament.

Such a trip was not to be undertaken lightly, and many hours planning and plotting a route kept Graham busy that winter. Doctor Doolittle, President of the Canadian Automobile Association, had driven a Model T Ford from coast to coast in 1925, but the car was equipped with steel railroad wheels to enable a safe run on the rail tracks, These steel wheels appear to have been a optional extra for the Model T

Graham gained valuable knowledge of the hazards the trip entailed in many meetings with Dr. Doolittle. The difference was Doolittle, and all others before him who were unsuccessful, had almost an expeditionary force with them. Graham was preparing for a solo journey, a lonely and prolonged test of his physical and mental skills, far from any human help and assistance for most of the ride. He rode the railway he was hoping to use as a road many times, to plot where he was to leave his fuel and oil dumps, as many of the rail halts did not possess roads of any description.

If the venture was to succeed, he had to enlist the assistance of the Canadian Railway Authorities, whose railway lines he would have to use to ride across the interior. They did not immediately take to the idea of a motorcycle using their rails, and it took many hours of persuasion by Graham and Castrol before they would entertain the idea. He had to attend the rail training school at Sault Ste. Marie, where he had to prove he could climb telephone poles (climbing irons provided) and show complete mastery of the field telephone. When the Canadian Pacific Railway later assented to the trip, Graham had to agree to a long list of conditions before they would allow him to ride their rails as an 'unscheduled freight train'.

By this time he had joined the staff of Conroy's, and through their dealership had persuaded Jack Sangster, then company secretary of Ariel Motor Co., to supply a 500 cc ohv single for the trip. Why did he choose an Ariel? Maybe it was the impression that marque made on Graham on his initial ride in Canada. Maybe because it was built by a large English manufacturer, big enough to sponsor such a madcap scheme. Graham had made contacts with the Selly Oak, Birmingham firm during his days at Burman, as Ariel used the Ryland Road gearboxes on all their range.

The machine chosen for the trip was the 497 cc 'Two Port' model, shown for the first time at the 1927 Olympia Show. With its new single down tube cradle frame and heavyweight Burman gearbox the machine had received critical acclaim from the motorcycling press. "Last year's Ariels were good machines, but the 1928 twin-port model is a very real advance on anything which the firm put on the market in 1927"

The Motor Cycle, June 28th, 1928

Graham wrote in his diary for this period.

"All preparations were gone ahead with and it was a happy day for me when the news came through from England stating that my machine had been despatched. I will gloss over the many days of suspense whilst the machine was on its way to Canada, day after day, and its non arrival made me worried and ill tempered. But at last, word came from the Custom authorities that it had landed. Get it up at once. No, don't wait for it to be delivered by ordinary method. Motor truck arranged and so it was carried in state to be assembled at our depot. Loving hands unpacked that machine, and I guarded it as a tiger over her cubs. "Leave that alone Johnnie, put that down Jimmie". A special bench was prepared and I was soon to be seen working silently and quickly building up the machine which was to be known as Toby and be destined to be the first vehicle to cross Canada on rubber tyres - I hope!"

His joy was short-lived when he discovered the speedo head had been stolen. An accurate reading was essential, especially for the railway portion of the journey, to ensure he kept to the timetable. Telegrams exchanged between Canada and England resulted in another instrument arriving.

"Days blended into nights but sleep was a secondary consideration to me. Was I not

J. V. & J. W. CONROY

Dominion Distributors of

ARIEL "THE MODERN CHOICE"
DOUGLAS "LEADER OF THE PACK"
ROYAL ENFIELD "MADE LIKE A GUN"
MOTORCYCLES

Showrooms
516 Danforth Ave.

Offices
408 Kent Building
TORONTO

Phones
Showrooms - GErrard 5762
Office   -   ADelaide 8854

Telegrams
"YORNOC" Toronto

Toronto July 14th. 1928

TO WHOM IT MAY CONCERN.

This is to certify that the bearer "Mr. J. Grahame Oates" is member of
the staff and represent's J.V. & J.W. Conroy. The Dominion Distributors
of the above mentioned products. At 516 Danforth Ave Toronto.

Mr. Oates has undertaken a Transcontinen
-tal Motor-Cycle trip from Atlantic to Pacific and back in order to
demonstrate the reliability of the machine he is riding "THE ALL BRITISH
ARIEL".

Any courtesies or assistance extended
Mr. Oates will be greatly appreciated by

J.V. Conroy. For.
J.V. & J.W. Conroy.

Specimen of Signature = J Graham Oates.

Aurora to Ariel   39   the motorcycling life of J. Graham Oates

working on my dear little Toby. At last all ready, tyres fitted with great care, kneegrips adjusted just so, handlebars placed to take the strain off my arms and the favourite Terry (saddle) adjusted to a degree for what of the hundreds of miles of spine shattering, body pounding ties of the Canadian railway. Gas, oil and now for the engine, a lusty kick and Toby starts for the first time on Canadian air. But I must take her gently for a few hundred miles in order to settle the bearing surfaces down to their work."

A nice gentle run to Hamilton, and it was there that the sidecar was fitted. This was a Sturgess, of Canadian manufacture. The sidecar body was made especially long, in order to provide sleeping accommodation for Graham throughout the trip. In view of the rough countryside to be crossed it had to have considerable ground clearance. Other than these alterations it was a standard sports model as supplied to the home market. The ride back to Toronto made him even keener to start the trip.

July 17th saw the outfit readied and after receiving the best wishes of his Toronto colleagues, and collecting letters from Mayor Mc Bride for his counterparts of Halifax and Vancouver he left for Halifax and the true start to the journey.

To assist the smooth running of the trip he had in his possession a letter from his employers J.V. & J.W. Conroy. It was signed by J.V. Conroy but - more important - he added his seal as a Justice of the Peace in the county of York, Ontario - friends in high places indeed!.

The original 1928 notebook has been made available from Graham's son, and I have used the entries where possible to let Graham's own words portray the pain and the pleasures he encountered on his attempt to be the first person to cross Canada by a rubber tyred motor vehicle. Very few dates have been appended to the entries, but I have indicated them where possible.

Graham's early haste to get to his starting point, Halifax, Nova Scotia, nearly led to disaster before the trip had begun.

"Monday night.

Started 8.30 from Toronto night time, had slight trouble with dynamo cut out sticking. Rectified matters and proceeded at about 30 through the night, machine running beautifully and night fine. Broke spot light lamp glass but do not need it on these good roads.

Driving downhill on a narrow road when I was suddenly confronted with a nasty looking corner. It was impossible to get round in safety, so I ran across someone's front garden where three children were playing. Their surprise at seeing me was unbounded and one little fellow did his utmost to imitate a monkey by attempting to climb the nearest apple tree! Roads unsafe for fast travel on high averages.

Saturday morning, 21st July 1928 and Toby and I are ready to go. The morning was taken up in having photographs taken, getting letters from the Mayor to hand to other Mayors on route, collecting my first pennant in order to have a collection from ocean to ocean on the completion of the trip. One o'clock and all was in readiness for the start."

Mayor Louis Gastonguay of Halifax filled a small bottle of water from the Atlantic Ocean and this was sealed and handed to Graham. He then shook hands with those present and allowed Toby to slide backwards down the slipway until the rear wheel was in the Atlantic. The Mayor made the following speech - *"I declare that this machine ridden by J. Graham Oates has been officially started by me after having placed the rear wheel in the Atlantic. In the event of Mr. Oates succeeding in being the first man to cross Canada by motor vehicle, I have requested that the Mayor of Vancouver similarly baptise the machine in the Pacific, and thus Mr. Oates will have completed the crossing from the Atlantic to the Pacific."*

"Had pictures taken. Bid Halifax bye bye and started kicking the gravel again. The roads were terrible and many times I had to lift my feet to prevent their being injured whilst crashing through the loose stones."

Another instance that again nearly scuppered the whole trip occurred on the evening of 22nd July. The diary notes:

"The day was very hot and the roads owing to lack of rain were very dusty. Passing cars was a positive nightmare and in order to keep my average speed I was called upon to take many long chances. Where I saw a straight road ahead and free from traffic, I let Toby go as fast as possible. During one of these fast interludes I saw a line of stones laid carelessly across the road about twelve inches apart. I attempted to

The start of an epic journey. Mayor Gastonguay of Halifax and Graham, with 'Toby' backed into the Atlantic Ocean at Halifax, Nova Scotia

use the brakes to pull up and the machine commenced to skid broadside. The road being narrow and high in the centre caused the outfit to make for the left hand ditch which certainly did not look exciting. It quickly occurred to me that it was impossible to prevent a crash and so I turned sharp left and hoped for the best. (The outfit was built with a right hand sidecar) To my great surprise the machine cleared the ditch and landed in a field. Not being satisfied with this it continued its mad plunge onwards, carrying down four fence posts and many feet of wire. I by this time was out of harm's way lying between the machine and sidecar and calculating how long it would take before we came to rest. Toby certainly displayed marvellous powers of absorbing punishment. After straightening out the mudguards and footrests and retrieving one knee grip which had been torn off by striking a pole, Toby, with the aid of a few fellow motorists was placed where she belonged and we again became good friends and continued with our fast ways.

My face was giving me a great deal of pain, it having been blistered and peeled by the combined efforts of sun, wind, and rain. It ached and I almost felt like taking a rest instead of a contemplated all night ride.

I was however determined on making Quebec my first stop for a

This photo is captioned 'Miss Boniface' in the scrapbook. Not sure if it refers to the town, or the young lady

well earned sleep. I stopped at Fredericton, New Brunswick for a meal in preparation for my night ride. Stories were told to me of the difficulties I would have in finding my way over the narrow roads which pass through hundreds of miles of the sportsman's paradise, the New Brunswick forests. I almost pitied myself as I left the warmth of the restaurant behind and rolled into flying suit and helmet. But I had a perfect little machine and good lights so hoped for a pleasant ride and the possible sight of the lordly moose, which are common sights in these forests. On into the dark and I remember I must shortly fill up my spare gas tins as I know there are no replenishment stations for many miles that keep open all night.

A small village trembles in the distance and in a very few minutes I drop down the winding road and into the gas station. Conversation is exchanged and having purchased some chocolate I kick Toby into life and steer again into the night. I am thankful for having good lights as the roads are narrow and winding. It is wonderful how a healthy engine keeps you company at night, mile after mile rolls along with steady monotony, until I glance at my illuminated handlebar watch which says midnight. Round a bend in the road and... heavens what is that hanging in the tree tops, mist as thick as soup. On go the brakes and we slow down to a crawl

Light shines ahead in long thin beams, but they are useless as they reflect the light back in to my already tired eyes. Ten miles an hour is the speed and even then it is not too safe. A wrench on the bars and I drag the outfit back on to the road out of a ditch which seemed very watery. Soon the rain has started in real earnest and very quickly the roads became like riverbeds, still Toby is game and we plunge on not seeing a living thing to break the loneliness of this terrific night journey. I am getting tired, my arms ache, my eyes are feeling the strain of the constant watch on the road ahead, and my face surely must be bleeding after having the rain smashing on it, every raindrop feels like a knife thrust. I feel my head drooping; heavens, surely I am not falling asleep, no that can't be. I know I have ridden for over thirty six hours without rest, but I have done that before. Bump. Damn, where am I. Silence, engine has stopped with a sudden jolt, and I am awake to find myself head on into a fence. No damage done thank goodness. I am pleased that the throttle shuts off when released, as I had fallen asleep on the machine and wandered right off the road.

No use going on, nature will not be denied. Spare gas, oil and person crawl in with my head in the front using a Castrol tin as a pillow. Sleep on pleasant dreams. Rrring, Yea Gods. Ooh., my head, as I rise in a hurry and forget where I am.

Damn and why did I ever think of this confounded across Canada trip. My neck feels as if the hangman had been putting in a little practice on me. My spine I swear will never be the same again and I am cold as well; never mind, I am. Those that have slept in a sidecar with the frame work as a mattress probably will agree with me that it needs a big stretch of imagination to include it under the word

comfort. However, I suppose it is permissible to grumble. The dawn is just breaking as I pack the last spare tin of gas into the sidecar and move off again. Everything seems fresh and sweet and the dust thank goodness does not trouble me.

Ah, the sun is going to shine soon and then all will be well. No, it is not; yes it is, as it peeps from behind a cloud. I soon feel its welcome warmth on my back and it encourages me to go faster in the hopes of getting within range of the bacon and egg smell. They say an army marches on its stomach, but I had never any desire to be an army. But to ride, and sway up and down on New Brunswick roads with your back bone making love to an empty stomach is not an enviable feeling"

This appears to be one of the very few times that he used the sidecar as a bed. He frequently stayed with gangs of railroad workers in their wayside huts when he was rail-riding, or cheap lodgings in small towns and hamlets he passed through.

Good progress was made through Nova Scotia, New Brunswick, Quebec, then through his 'adopted home' province of Ontario to Sault Ste. Marie (known to Canucks as the Soo), where he was to first take to the rails of his 900 mile railroad ride. The first railway he had to traverse was the Algoma Central Railway, but it appears from his diary that he had overlooked the necessity to gain permission to ride their rails. Possibly all railways came under the Canadian Pacific Railway network, but they had simply failed to notify the Algoma Co. they were due to have a three-wheeled petrol-powered vehicle using the lines. After being held up for three days he was only given the go-ahead after they contacted the powers to be at the CPR. The Algoma Central Railway was

The scrapbook reads "I always move over for these!" Schreiber, Ontario

chiefly used at that time to ship iron ore from Wawa on eastern Lake Superior south to the Algoma Steel Co. blast furnaces at Sault Ste. Marie.

"Sun and wind very tiring to my face which looks more like a cherry and is so sore that the slightest rain spells agony.

Left Toronto in fine weather and started second stage of my trip. Not feeling very well *but carried on, bike not steering nicely owing to link bolt being inactive. Bad rain and mist just before getting into North Bay. Left [North Bay] in terrific downpour, rain, rain and nothing but squish, squish through holes deep in water, clouds of steam but little engine never falters, thank goodness for the dope I put on the terminals. Road under water at times, many car crashes on the terrible skiddy black mud in that part of the country. "Jesus is the only one that can save," said a sign on a corner which I nearly fell over. Got into ditch and had to drag Toby out by brute force.*

Left Sudbury for the Soo, very dusty and roads bad, nearly fell off the road looking at good fishing water, had puncture and other sorts of trouble, got to Soo at 7.

Now the trouble starts."

Outside of the station Graham slotted Toby between the rails. The outfit fitted quite neatly between them, and it was a bone-shaking trip along the sleepers that Graham took. Early on he found to his cost that rain culverts had a very diverting effect on the machine - especially when hit at speed. Just 150 kms into the rail ride and he came upon his first major obstacle. This was the bridge that spanned the Montreal River, a large wooden trestle type that took the railroad 263 ft. above the foaming river. The rails lay over widely spaced cross members that would have swallowed the Ariel's 26 x 3.25 -inch wheels whole. The trip appeared doomed at this point but Graham was not to be beaten. He strapped on the climbing spikes and scaled the nearest telephone pole and clipped on his field telephone.

The next train that arrived at the Montreal Bridge delivered to our stranded traveller two wide boards about 3 yds. long. After making

The railway took its toll on the exhaust pipes. The Great Divide, Crowsnest Pass, Alberta

certain that no further trains were due for the rest of the day, Graham laid the first board between the rails, put the sidecar wheel on a rail and edged the outfit out over the river. The second board was laid in front and the step was repeated over and over to get the outfit safely to the other side, the operation taking Graham all day.

All through the trip he was in constant contact with the railway company via the telephone. They gave advance warning so that reporters for the local press were aware of his impending arrival. The news of his bridge crossing episode made the national papers and, two days after this feat, he was tracked down by the Fox newsreel company, who asked if he would care to go back and repeat the feat for the cameras. The first reaction was unprintable - but mindful of the coverage it would give his sponsors, Graham agreed to repeat part of the bridge crossing. The company took him and Toby back to the Montreal Bridge on a railway flatcar, the last few feet were repeated and he was then delivered back from whence they found him to continue his journey.

This first rail ride was a severe test of man, machine and sidecar. Graham suffered much bruising from the incessant crashing over the ties, and the bike gave clutch trouble, so it needed re-corking many times through the trip. At one point the railway dispatched a clerk to their local drug store for a large bag of corks. This was sent through to Graham when the next train passed him. The exhaust pipes did not stand pounding the rails for long, and in no time they were flattened so Graham simply sawed them off leaving just short pipes pointing straight down to the ground.

The Sturgess sidecar gave trouble right from the start. Early in the trip the sidecar stub axle broke and Graham was forced to ride 14 miles with the sidecar chassis skidding on the rail until he got to an air base of the Ontario Dept. of Lands and Forest, who used seaplanes for patrol against forest fires. They airlifted him back to their workshop at the Soo where three stronger axles were made from a half shaft.

At Schreiber, Ontario, Graham was invited to meet the President of the Canadian Pacific Railway. This was their first meeting, although Graham - and Castrol had corresponded many times in their bid to get the permission needed to ride the rails. Mr. Beattie was obviously curious to meet this character who had put his case so forcefully and with such commitment that he gave permission. Graham limped into the meeting with Mr. Beattie, who queried whether he had been injured. No, was the reply, it was simply that the heel of his shoe had disappeared somewhere along the line! Graham's shoe was taken away and re-heeled whilst they ate a hearty meal together.

The chassis and connections also needed continual attention and 17 miles from Franz, it finally broke free from the machine. Graham rode into Franz solo, and the sidecar was delivered to him by train the next day, but only after he paid 3 dollars freightage on it. At Franz he left the Algoma Railway and took to the Canadian Pacific Railway lines. He was diverted off the track at White Bridge when the train with Prince George on board came into the station. The Prince spotted the machine but Graham was unable to get a chat with him.

The ride took him along the banks of Lake Superior, and it was along this stretch that the machine dropped off the lines and nearly ended up in the Lake. When Graham got down to the shore to collect it he had to beat a hasty retreat; the outfit had come to rest very adjacent to a

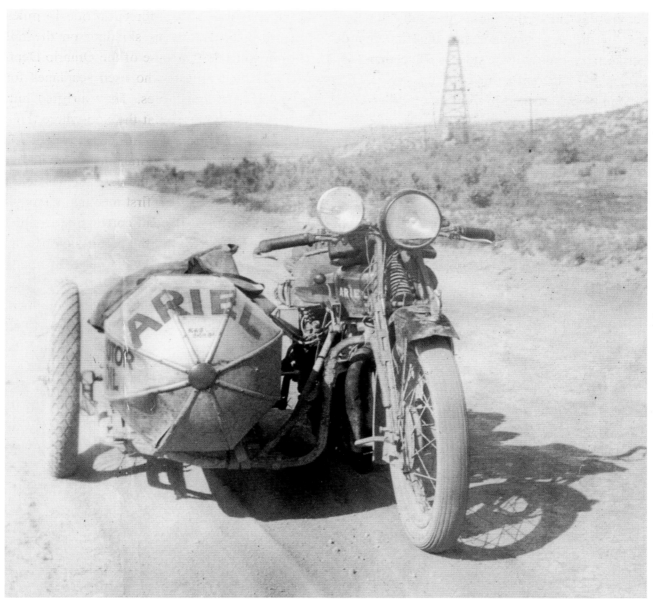

hornets nest and its occupants were a trifle unsettled! When it was safe to retrieve Toby, he had to manhandle it a quarter of a mile back to the track over rock, through bushes, and small streams.

The trip was not a race against time, so Graham was able to take many rest and recreation days throughout the trip, and one such was an invitation to go to Sand Lake for a few days.

"Rain, rain most unpleasant. Black flies and mosquitos. The waiting is unbearable so accepted invitation to go to Sand Lake, misnamed, should be Lake of Flies but possessing compensation inasmuch as it possesses a girls camp. I stayed a few days enjoying camp life in a wonderful manner and I was only sorry to leave."

The rail track crew and the Ontario Provincial Police came to his rescue many times when it was just impossible to get the 600 lb. outfit back on the tracks by himself. Despite this, the journey was not all troublesome, and Graham spent many happy hours shooting, fishing, and hunting on the trip, either alone or with the Mounties, or the track crew.

"Bad road bed and bridges bump teeth out, arms ache and eyes watching ties.

Everyone just splendid, taking meal in Fire Depots shack.

Received letters, feeling fed up with the whole trip, have gone through hell and yet I seem to have done nothing and no person seems to be interested.

Left Port Arthur for Winnipeg, passed through scenery very like I.O.M. Broke another (sidecar) spindle which marred an otherwise enjoyable run.

With feelings of great regret I got again onto the lines for the last stretch of 75 miles to White."

As the days passed, miles passed under Toby's wheels and he finally made Whitemouth, Manitoba where he was able to leave the rails behind and take once more to the roads, after 900 miles of rail riding. A trip from Lands End to John O'Groats is approximately 800 miles, so Graham drove further than this between the rail lines.

As if the rails were not enough, Graham then encountered miles and miles of 'gumbo' - a glutinous Canadian mud that stuck to all and everything. Eventually all three mudguards were removed for this part of the trip to help the wheels rotate.

The never ending flat prairie lands of Manitoba, Saskatchewan, and Alberta were traversed in fair time in a mixture of mud, dust, chassis repairs, and an increasing number of punctures. Driving across the prairies is a frustrating experience today, so it must have seemed to take a lifetime for Graham and the outfit, with the west wind in his teeth all the time. Even when the Rockies came into view they didn't seem to be getting any closer, which was an optical illusion since they can be seen from so far off.

At Winnipeg he took a week's rest from his labours to recharge his batteries and also check the machine over. It had been difficult to sleep on the journey, as every time he closed his eyes he could see a train bearing down on him! It was at the picture house that he saw the film that had been taken at the Montreal River Bridge.

"Saw the cinema of self crossing the famed Bridge. Scenery beautiful and altogether a good picture, rode into the camera and faded out in the distance after having stopped to light cigarette and then rode on. Not a movie star by a long shot"

It at first appeared that all footage of the newsreel film had disappeared without trace, but diligent work by the Canadian National Museum archivists came up with a 30 second clip. Regrettably, the nitrate stock had deteriorated very badly, so only a scant three seconds is viewable.

Even though Graham took every opportunity to replace the tyres, he was still plagued by punctures. In one instance he was forced to stuff the rear cover with grass and leaves when he found the tyre pump had bounced out of the sidecar.

The media coverage Graham received cover many pages of his huge scrapbook, and by now he was getting moral assistance from many motorcycle clubs he encountered as he neared his goal. Approaching Calgary he had his first sight of the Rockies, the fulfillment of a promise he made to himself at the Douglas Picture House in 1919.

In Calgary he ran into a ditch missing a

runaway horse and cracked the frame. The engine was beginning to protest at the cruel treatment it had endured. For the whole of the rail ride the bike never used top gear and third gear was used very infrequently, the quicker he went the more chance there was of an accident! He bumped back onto the rail lines to traverse the Rockies. By now the lighting system had given up the ghost, so a large car battery was borrowed to illuminate the rails ahead of him as he passed through the 8 mile Revelstoke Tunnel.

By now it was a daily habit to repair the sidecar chassis, and he must have trebled its weight with the added braze, weld and steel bars inserted in the tubes. Tyres and chains were changed when available - or repaired when not.

As Graham reached the outskirts of Vancouver on the evening of the 21st September, a stone jammed in the primary chain and nearly pitched him off.

As he approached Vancouver he was flagged down by two motorcycle policemen. The Mayor, Louis D. Taylor was keen to join Graham on the final leg of the journey, so all Graham's travelling possessions were transferred to the limousine and he rode on to the Town Hall with a mayoral passenger. After dining with Vancouver dignitaries the Mayor was re-installed in the sidecar and they took the trip down to English Bay, Vancouver where Mayor Taylor complied with the wishes of Mayor Louis Gastonguay and baptised the machine in the Pacific on 22nd September.

Journeys end. Mayor Taylor and Graham at English Bay, Vancouver

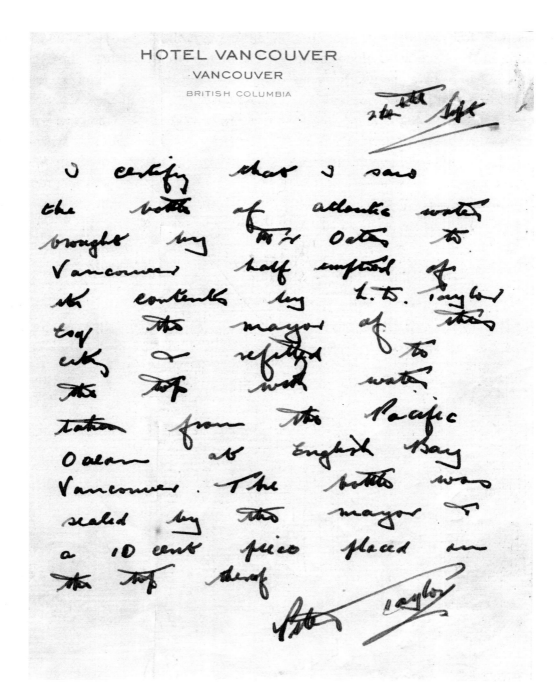

HOTEL VANCOUVER

VANCOUVER

BRITISH COLUMBIA

The bottle of 'Atific' water was mounted on a wooden plinth with a plaque bearing the following message.

First crossing Canada on rubber tyres Halifax Nova Scotia to Vancouver BC Graham Oates June to September 1928

Regrettably, the bottle of 'Atific' water has been smashed.

After 4027 miles and 21 riding days the journey was over at last, Graham had achieved the ride of a lifetime. Now all he had to do was turn round and ride home again.

What had been merely an expedition with considerable company and resources for Dr Doolittle, was, for Graham a lonely and prolonged test of his physical and mental skills.

It is impossible for anyone who has not travelled alone in the Canadian wilderness to realize what it is like to be alone and far from any human help or assistance.

Adverts placed by Ariel Motors in the British and Canadian motorcycle press suggest that the whole trip was covered without the slightest hint of mechanical malaise - the truth was very different. In the diary, mention is made of rail carriage for the freightage of a frame, and it may be that he changed the frame in Vancouver before the trip back.

Unwilling to endure another rail ride and miles of gumbo, Graham took the return route back to Toronto by dropping down to the United States where there were major highways all the way, but even so it was no easy journey. The tired motor failed many limes on the return journey, and in one 36 hour stretch he had to strip the motor out three limes. Broken valves and valve guides were replaced with modified Chevrolet items, the timing side main bearing bush failed, causing the oil pump to fail, and he was forced to cut new ring grooves in the piston. More than once he was forced to sit by the roadside and rebuild the engine with his own spanners, having been denied the use of tools by automobile repair shops.

Approaching Laramie, Wyoming, the highway climbed to 9,800 ft., which proved the undoing of the tired Ariel engine, and the summit was reached on the back end of a tow

Holding the damaged wheel together, Pocatello, Idaho

rope. The magdyno needed attention to the windings on two consecutive days, and when the sidecar tyre shredded itself at Pocatello, Idaho, Graham bound the remnants to the rim with strong rope until he got to the next large town. There he had to rebuild the wheel with an American gauge rim as no suitable tyre was available in America for the original Canadian one.

He found the American attitude to motorcyclists much less friendly than he was used to and had experienced in Canada, and was grateful to finally re-enter Canada at the Detroit / Ontario border, where a group of his British Empire Motor Club mates escorted him the last few miles back home.

A visit to England on a promotional and business trip was combined with a trip to the Island on an Ariel combination loaned by the Selly Oak firm. The temptation to climb Snaefell via the railway was too much. It was a successful attempt even though Graham threw Dennis Browne, - the Canadian Castrol man - out of the chair when they hit a rain culvert!

Members of the British Empire Motor Club line up with Graham and the Conroy staff after the trans-Canada trip

Chapter 4

OVERSEAS MOTORS - WORLD MOTOR BOAT ENDURANCE RECORD - THE BRITISH EMPIRE MOTOR CLUB

After that pioneering Trans-Canada trip, Graham changed employers to take over the Vice Presidency of a new motorcycle dealership, Overseas Motors Ltd. 133 Danforth Avenue, Toronto, Ontario, run by Jack Heath, another British emigre. Overseas Motors originally held the agencies for Rudge-Whitworth, Matchless, and Coventry Eagle, but very soon added the Ariel franchise - no doubt due to Graham's presence. In addition to motorcycles they held agencies for radios and motor boats including the Dunelt, built by the motorcycle firm of Dunfold & Elliott from Birmingham, as well as the locally produced Johnson outboard motor boats.

The Canadian motorcyclist in the late 20s was not favoured by the police, and any cases of speeding and reckless riding were severely dealt with. It was not hard to prove a charge of speeding when the open road speed limit of the time was only 35 mph, and it would be asking too much for the sporting lads on their lightweight British singles not to try their mounts for speed. It was not unheard of for them to try and outrun the odd constable mounted mostly on 1,300 cc Henderson fours. Sam Rogers, another Manx emigre recalls one such case. He had been into court on a speeding charge and the magistrate Wm. Keith had observed to Sam, "If you don't know the rules of the road you should not have a motorcycle!" before fining him $25 with costs against him.

As Sam left the dock he espied Graham making his way in. Comparing notes, they found that both had been collared by Provincial Officer G. Hallick, but Graham was convinced that he could talk his way out of any fine, even though he had led the officer a merry dance that day, mounted on a 1,000 cc Coventry Eagle, possibly the model powered by the Anzani V-twin motor.

Sam thought otherwise, so he nipped round to the public gallery just as Graham entered the dock. Very soon Graham had launched into his defence, regaling the Judge with the facts that as an Isle of Man TT and trans-Canada rider, he was far more in control of his machine than the officer, who probably had a far more limited experience in the control of a motorcycle. Regrettably the soliloquy had a reverse effect on magistrate Wm Keith, who not only fined him the mandatory $25 and costs, but cancelled his driver's permit for two months as well!

Around this time the British Empire Motor Club was formed in Toronto, and Graham was elected first President. He always proudly carried the B.E.M.C. badge on his machines. This club was formed to fly the flag for British machines against the tide of the larger V-twin American imports, Harley Davidson, Excelsior, Indian etc., with no allegiance to any dealer or make of motorcycle. A rider of an Indian was shunned by Harley Davidson riders and vice versa. The B.E.M.C. was a more friendly club with all British riding motorcyclists being made most welcome. The events run by the B.E.M.C. were formulated to favour the lighter, more nimble British roadsters. The club, which still exists, organised many long-distance events, even 24 hour races held on public roads. They were in fact part trials, part scrambles over the dirt roads and tracks, but full of incident as the nimbler British bikes often beat their cumbersome American rivals.

These events in the early 30s used a 20 mile course, and it was a mass start at 5 p.m. and continued until 5 p.m. the next day - or until the last competitor retired. Changes of rider and passenger were allowed, and when Graham won the 45 cubic-inch class in the first 24-hour race, run in the Caledon Hills on the Ariel, he wore out three passengers. He had the inevitable electrical trouble, as first the battery fell off and then the dynamo stopped charging, forcing him to tag onto the rear light of a big Harley through the dust at dusk. Dirt track racing was all the rage and Graham was well equipped with a 500 Rudge he used, both solo and sidecar, and a Mk l KTT Velocette.

The Club's first headquarters were at Overseas Motors and they tried very hard in their early days to improve the image of motorcycling, even as far as designing and making corporate club riding gear.

Whether it was to show how poor he was, or that he did not want to get the club into trouble, when Graham went before the judge to contest his speeding conviction, he was dressed rather shabbily, contrary to the 'posh' image the B.E.M.C. was trying to cultivate.

To promote the boat division of the Overseas Motors' business - and Castrol - Graham undertook to try and set an outboard motor boat world record on Clear Lake, Ontario, with an Imperial model Johnson Standard Runabout, powered by a Sea Horse 32 hp motor in June 1930. The motor for the attempt was run in and tuned in the back yard of Overseas Motors, much to the annoyance of their neighbours who rather objected to the 4 cylinder motor being run flat out attached to a 45 gallon oil drum in the back yard.

Graham's inexperience in matters maritime caused some of the spectators at the lake to have qualms about the wisdom of trying such a record attempt, but the pilot was confident so

Graham pilots 'Miss Wynne' on Clear Lake, Ontario. The large splash adjacent to 'Miss Wynne' is Bill King leaping off after refuelling

the record effort was on. The run started well but, just over twelve hours into the attempt, just when it was getting dusk, Graham spotted a large log floating in the lake. To continue with such hazards at night would have been suicidal so he had no option but to call a halt to the run. By this time new record figures had been set up for the 6 and 12 hour.

The 24 hour attempt was rescheduled for July 18th, and Graham had to retrace those initial twelve hours and then continue onwards for the full 24 hours; daylight came and went, and 'Miss Wynne', as he named the little boat, only faltered once when the fuel line became choked. Graham was fed with soggy sandwiches and hot chocolate throughout the trip. After 12 hours Graham briefly fell asleep, and the boat grounded off the shallows at the South Beach. He wrenched the wheel round to pull 'Miss Wynne' back into the deep channel. This made the timing officials fear for his safety, but it also had the effect of bringing Graham wide awake.

The refuelling procedure, which was carried out every six hours, was original. Two companions, Don Wood and Bill King, chased Graham in a speed boat, and when they were

"More petrol and Horlicks" Bill and Don head off for a refuelling rendezvouz

alongside tins of fuel were transferred over and one climbed on board to refuel the tanks. When the refuelling was complete the refueller jumped back over the side, using the empty fuel cans as buoyancy aids, to be collected by the pursuing speed boat - all the while Graham was chasing his wake round and round the lake. The constant engine note made him temporarily deaf so the timekeepers had to write him notes to ensure that he knew how the attempt was going. At 9.15 p.m. he cut the motor and stepped ashore to be greeted with the news that he had beaten his own 6 and 12 hour records, in addition he had covered 292 miles at an average of 20.48 miles an hour. This effort set up a

The Castrol man mixes the petroil

Deaf! but a world record holder

Telegrams 'CASTROL,TORONTO.'
Telephone: ADELAIDE 5331
Codes: BENTLEY'S & PRIVATE.

BY APPOINTMENT
TO
THEIR EXCELLENCIES

THE GOVERNOR-GENERAL
AND
VISCOUNTESS WILLINGDON

BY APPOINTMENT TO H. M. THE KING

LORD WAKEFIELD OF HYTHE
GOVERNING DIRECTOR.

MANAGER FOR CANADA
CHARLES D. BROWNE

BY APPOINTMENT TO
H.M. THE KING OF SPAIN

C. C. Wakefield & Co., Limited.

MANUFACTURERS OF HIGH CLASS LUBRICANTS.

80 KING ST. WEST

HEAD OFFICES:
WAKEFIELD HOUSE,
CHEAPSIDE, LONDON.

**BRANCHES
AND
AGENCIES.**

Home.

ABERDEEN,	GLASGOW,
BELFAST,	LEEDS,
BIRMINGHAM,	LIVERPOOL,
CARDIFF,	MANCHESTER,
CORK,	NEWCASTLE-ON-TYNE,
DONCASTER,	NOTTINGHAM,
DUBLIN,	RUGBY.
DUNDEE,	

Canada.

MONTREAL,	TORONTO,
WINNIPEG,	REGINA,
SASKATOON,	LETHBRIDGE,
CALGARY,	EDMONTON,
VANCOUVER,	VICTORIA.

Abroad.

ADELAIDE,	MADRAS,
ADEN,	MADRID,
AUCKLAND,	MALMO,
BANGKOK,	MARSEILLES,
BARCELONA,	MALTA,
BATAVIA,	MELBOURNE,
BELGRADE,	MILAN,
BERLIN,	MONTEVIDEO,
BLANTYRE,	NAIROBI,
BOMBAY,	NELSON,
BRISBANE,	NEW YORK,
BRUSSELS,	OSLO,
BUCHAREST,	PALERMO,
BUDAPEST,	PARIS,
BUENOS AIRES,	PENANG,
BULAWAYO,	PERTH.(W.A.)
CAIRO.	PORT ELIZABETH,
CALCUTTA,	PORT HERALD,
CAPE TOWN,	PORT SUDAN,
CHRISTCHURCH,	PRAGUE,
COLOGNE,	RANGOON,
COLOMBO,	SANTOS,
COPENHAGEN,	SAO PAULO,
DRAMMEN,	SEMARANG,
DUNEDIN,.	SINGAPORE,
DURBAN.	SOURABAYA,
EAST LONDON.	SYDNEY,
FREETOWN.	
GENEVA.	
HELSINGFORS	
JOHANNESBU	
KAMPALA.	
KARACHI.	
KHARTOUM.	
KINGSTON (JAMAI	
LAS PALMA	
LIMA,	
LISBON,	

PLEASE QUOTE
OUR REF: CDB:L.
YOUR REF:

Toronto. July 25th, 1930.

J. Graham Oates, Esq.,
The Overseas Motors, Ltd.,
133 Danforth Ave.,
TORONTO, Ont.

My dear Graham:-

      With reference to our conversation of the other day, I cabled London as suggested by you, and this morning the following reply was received:

    "We are informed there is no official record."

      This refers to the 24-hour outboard displacement runabout boat record.

      You therefore, apparently, have the World's Record.

      Good luck to you.

      Yours faithfully,

"CASTROL" (Regd) MOTOR OILS

Membership Certificate 208
NATIONAL YACHT CLUB
TORONTO, CANADA
1-9-3-0

NAME J. G. Oates
COMMODORE Hemmings SECRETARY H. Jenkins
THIS TICKET MUST BE PRESENTED ON REQUEST OF OFFICERS

Aurora to Ariel   56   the motorcycling life of J. Graham Oates

world 24 hour outboard record for the first time.

This appears to have been his only foray into aquatic record breaking, but the next year he drove a Pontiac 6 for over 3,000 miles in 7 days with the oil filler sealed. This was not a speed record, but to demonstrate that Castrol lubricants would work efficiently for that length of time. The route for this trip was Toronto to Halifax and back without the engine stopping. His co-driver on this trip was Eric Chitty, who was later to make the journey across to England to find fame and fortune there as a speedway rider, as Captain of West Ham, and also three-times British Speedway Champion.

In Canada he gave many talks about the TT and persuaded the British Empire Motor Club to hold a series of races to find a suitable rider to send to the Island. H.S. Green rode a Rudge in the 1932 Senior TT, but managed to complete only four laps before, in removing his fly-smeared goggles to get better vision, he was struck in the eye by a bee and was forced to retire. At the time he was 28 minutes down on Stanley Woods.

At this time all British motorcycles sold into Canada were subject to an import tax, yet despite this, Canada was the only colonial territory that increased its share of machine sales in 1931. Graham saw there was a golden opportunity to increase these figures even more if he could get the tax repealed. Until 1926, the Canadian import tariff on American motorcycles was 35%, on British 22.5%. From April, 1926 until 1932 it was 20% on American and 12.5% on British.

Graham with the Pontiac 6

H S Green, B.E.M.C. entrant in the 1932 Senior TT

THE EARLY HISTORY OF THE BRITISH EMPIRE MOTOR CLUB

The following are articles on the foundation and early years of the British Empire Motor Club. The first was written by the then Club President Johnny Edmonston. The second was written by Gerald Barker, a long-time friend of Graham Oates.

To some of our newer members these remarks and ramblings may help them to understand the B.E.M.C., its objects and aims a little better and to allay some of the antipathy regarding the m/cycle section and why we seem to cater quite a lot to the motorcycles in this club who are far out of proportion to the actual membership today.

Today the tail wags the dog in the B.E.M.C. and for myself I can only see this as an inevitable conclusion to the times and economic situation. This, I do feel is a bad condition of affairs and I find that I, personally, get as much fun out of the cars as I ever did out of my motorcycling past and, if you delve into the heart of a lot of our car membership you would find a great number of ex-motoryclists.

This club was founded in 1928 by a group of five who rode English bikes in a country predominately American in thought and outlook, with the Harley and Indian dealers being the organisers and leaders of two rival factions erroneously called clubs.

My first competitive event in 1928, was a mud run with turkeys as prizes. Two friends and I entered and finished well up. I placed second. When the Indian dealer saw my name up there on the prize list he protested loud and very vigorously and I found myself demoted a place on the list and he to second.

We thought this was a trifle unfair and if this

was the state of affairs we decided it would be better for us to form a new club and to operate along British club lines. We chose the rather grandiose name of "The British Empire Motor Club" to draw to ourselves a little better type of motorcyclist who was interested in good sport and try and improve the present condition on the game. At that time we were far-sighted enough to call it a motor club, never at any time visualizing the tremendous club and sports car movement it has developed into.

At one time we had quite a group of motorboat enthusiasts in the club and our first President was Jimmy Oates.

All in all he was a wonderful first President and a good starter for some of the marvelous characters the club has known over the years. Dennis Griffin, our first Secretary, was another Grand Type. He was the brother-in-law to the well-known George Stevens of A.J.S. fame. I will never forget Dennis going to business (he was a banker by profession) in a derby hat, black coat and striped trousers astride a 37 cu. in. Indian dirt job.

I can assure you that Dennis stopped traffic

*The first B.E.M.C. 24-hour race,
starting at Belfountain in the
Caledonian Hills.
Top: Starting off
Centre:
Bottom: J G O winner of the 45
cubic-inch class*

at King and Bay Streets. Dennis later went back to England and became a staff writer for The Motorcycle, writing some very fine articles and road tests and always giving the B.E.M.C. and Canada a good boost.

We rode anything those days. The clubs first official event was a grass track-cum-scramble for a church at Scarboro. I never knew that fellows could come off and on their bikes as fast and as often as we did in one day. We also had a soccer team on m/cycles and challenged all-comers, but did not receive too many acceptances to any challenge. I believe that we were considered slightly eccentric at that time.

Around this time Bill Drury joined our club. Bill was a fairly wealthy type and could ride motorcycles, drive a car (he had the first Reo Flying Cloud I had ever seen) and he also flew his own plane (a Curtiss Robin). Bill won the Windsor- Los Angeles air derby in 1928 flying a WACO. He was also one of the finest beer drinkers the club has ever had on its roster. Bill used to fly into town from St. Catherines and drive a Henderson and sidecar outfit for P.A. m/cycles in dirt track events, occasionally switching to an Ariel. He owned the first Brough Superior 100SS ever in Canada.

One of our early events was a challenge sidecar versus solo event on a dirt track with Bill and the Henderson, Jimmy Oates and the Ariel and myself as sidecar passenger at Eden in the Caledonian Hills. That was one of the hairiest affairs I have ever been in and though one lost to the solos, our performance that evening was terrific.

Along around the end of 1928 we conceived the idea of a 24-hour trial and in 1929 we were able to get the roads closed at Belfountain in the Caledonian Hills. We had a circle course up the mountain and down with only one mile of paved road. We started at 4 p.m. on the Sunday afternoon and rode for the full 24 hours keeping

Graham's Rudge dirt track outfit; Eric Chitty in the saddle

A complimentary club to the B.E.M.C. The British Motorcycle Club, Vancouver

an average speed that was quite high. Have you ever ridden a motorcycle for that length of time over back country roads with hump-back bridges and railway tracks? Believe me my 'derriere' was pounded badly and I don't think it ever did get back to its pristine shape again. It was here that I first met Jim Fergusson. About 4 a.m. I was bouncing down the mountain side when I came upon Jim in the ditch. I guess he had fallen asleep. I helped where I could and we got him going again but his A.J.S. was too badly bent to finish. If I recall it right Jim joined the B.E.M.C. after that and it was the start of a friendship that has lasted a long time with very little strain on either of us.

Is this the event that we rode part of the route under the railway bridge on our first visit?

To Jim went the honour of having the first sports car in the Club. This was a fearsome MG 14/40 1928 vintage with inflatable seats which I soon found held no air in them, or ever would. I

imagine that Jim felt that any m/c type or girlfriend of such a type did not need air cushions to ride on, and many's the back country road we covered in agony over chasing some 'will o' the wisp' clue in a club treasure hunt. I don't ever remember Jim slowing down for anything once we were headed for the next clue.

You know, over the years we've had some wonderful stout-hearted girl friends and wives who helped us along and the B.E.M.C. should some day (when we get a permanent club house) unveil a plaque in honour of the fine efforts of some of the 'Gals' we've known and then married. Its wonderful, and as I wander around Harewood, Hockley and the Winter Rally I am assuming that the breed has changed. NONE AT ALL.

Our earliest efforts were towards upgrading the sport and to this end we introduced events such as a scramble based on the old Scott Trial *idea. We were able to organize a very presentable event in the Don Valley and later at Weston near the Kodak plant. This type of event was a complete change and surprise to the local lads and quite a few saw that a new era had begun in motorcycling in the Toronto area.*

B.E.M.C., ever truly a club of 'firsts' and, I believe that today that tradition still lives with us. We organised the first long-distance trail with observed sections and the time element entering in only a minor part. The premium being placed on riding, it wasn't long before the old sloppy, dashing, leg-waving riding was giving way to neatness and skill. We also decided that the average local motorcyclist looked like a 'BUM' to us, so we agreed to do something about it. We went to a tailor and had

suits of plus-fours made up. Boy, were we DOGS. We all adopted pipe smoking and we must have looked quite a sight to the locals when we rode down the streets with our pipes puffing furiously and sparks flying behind us.

About 1929 Jimmy Oates managed to talk the Castrol Oil Co. into presentation of a beautiful trophy (the first good one in the club) and so the Castrol Trial became an annual event with us, only discontinued during the War. With the advent of this trophy and the competition between oil companies being keen in Canada, we soon acquired the Shell Trophy and this became an annual event too. In all the years I rode, I only got my name on that trophy once and never on the 'Castrol'. I guess I was no Vic Brittain.

'Hillclimbing'

1929 saw Jack Fisher join us. The gang used to meet at Overseas Motors, Danforth Avenue and we heard this rich type was getting a Sunbeam. To us Ariel and A.J.S. types this could only mean that a millionaire had moved in. By some chance when the new bike arrived I was delegated to teach 'Fish' how to ride. I showed him how things worked, etc., and said "now go and do your stuff" - so 'Fish' started off in low gear and in the space of three or four yards he had the bike in high gear. The heart-rending noises from that beautiful engine in high gear made me moan in agony. There was I running after 'Fish' down what is now O'Connor Drive screaming and cursing at him. He soon caught on and I had another B.E.M.C. member in the fold. 'Fish' has been a wonderful servant to the Club for a long time now. Certainly our money has never been as jealously guarded and in the days when the treasury showed 75 cents it was as clearly and as carefully reported as out thousands of dollars are today.

Early in 1928 we got real ambitious and decided we needed a high-grade race meet of some kind, so we had a club run to Wasaga Beach. The beach was in good shape and we had a good bash before the police arrived. Some of the locals saw the possibilities and we started to negotiate with the authorities. The Beach itself being a Highway made it tough for us and it wasn't until 1935 that we were able to put on our first meet. The enthusiasm was terrific and we used the Kaye Don Trophy as our premium award. 1935 was one of those great depression years and how we managed to raise funds to organize an event of this size, I don't know. It was mostly blood, sweat, toil and tears. I added a few curses too. I was competition convenor at that time and the delays were awful. We set a date for the October holiday but a great political shemozzle was in the making that Fall and the holiday was put off by the government so the election could take place. We eventually got a date around the 28th October.

To get the beach closed for one day to

Indian riders on Wasaga Beach, 1935. The centre rider is Don Eby

conduct the races we had to put up two miles of snow fence, supplied by the Highway department, and we could not start this until the morning of the race. A chap called Harry Ashton left with me on my bike at 3.30 a.m. from Toronto and when we reached Barrie it started to snow. We ran that event in a wet snow storm, and on the way into the beach Harry and I were knocked off the bike into a ditch by the farmer's truck. Harry had very poor sight and the bounce into the ditch caused him to lose his glasses and he also had concussion. Poor old 'Ash' never saw a race that day. Surprisingly, we had a very good crowd and the races went off very well. Competitors, organisers, wives and girlfriends and anybody we could 'Joe' into a job pitched in to put that two miles of fence up, handle the crowd, lap score and see the riders got on the line on time. We had a ball, and the satisfaction of putting a few dollars in the treasury from a collection taken by the girls, I remember at that time our membership list never reached the hundred mark, but we believed that's why you join a club, its having fun with all the gang, waving a flag and helping in any capacity whatsoever.

Winner of our first Wasaga Beach 100-mile race was Mat Goldhart on a Harley Davidson but this was only after Tony Miller with his Ariel had led the race for practically the whole distance. Incidentally Tony won the beach race in 1937 and 1938, being the only two-time winner of the Kaye Don trophy. A note of interest here, the winner of the 500 c.c. standard class was Len Norris, the famous cartoonist of the Vancouver Sun, on a Triumph.

Wasaga was not our first major event. In 1931 we were able to persuade North York Council to close the Post Road and Bridle Path off Bayview Avenue for a race meet and this was the first time a public road had been closed for a high-speed race meet. This was a really

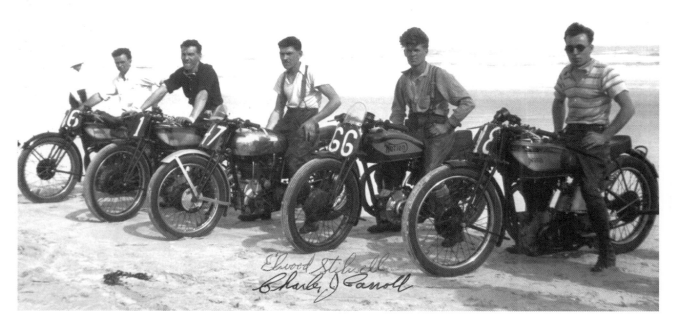

B.E.M.C. members at Daytona. Left to right: Clark Trumbull, Washington, DC, (placed 2nd on Norton), Tony Miller (whose Norton put a rod through the cases), Bryan Sparks, Windsor on his HRD Vincent TT model, Elwood Stillwell, London on his '31 Norton, Chuck Carroll, Windsor.

perfect course of about 1½ miles. We ran three classes in the first event and Eddie Hughes, a Northern Ireland type, won the 350 c.c. and 500 c.c. events on a 350 c.c. 4-valve Rudge. Ed went to the Isle of Man TT in 1932 to represent Canada in our reciprocal deal with the ACU which our club at a time represented. The Bayview TT did not last long and in 1932 saw the last race there. Winners in 1932 were 250 c.c. Harold Hunter on a beautiful 250 camshaft OK Supreme. Harold was a cracking good rider and a very good tuner, and you sports types will know him as the designer of that 2-cam head on Jim Ferguson's Healey 100SS that Roly Keith drove so fast at Vancouver last year.

Around that time, dirt track racing was a big part of our sport. We used to practice of an evening, we also had a very dangerous third of a mile track at Stuesville and in the east end of the city we had Ulster Stadium, a quarter-mile track on the football field. We had some good riders in these events who later became big names in the dirt-track events in England. Cordy Milne and his brother and Eric Chitty (a club member from Toronto) who later became captain of West Ham speedway and World Champion for three years. Eric was the first rider I had seen in Canada who would ride anything, anywhere at any time - I TAUGHT HIM!

Jim Ferguson, Chitty and a few more club members ran a sort of barn-storming group around the Northern States speedway circuits and made quite a name for themselves and carried the B.E.M.C. flag to a lot of places. Also about this time the famous Daytona Beach races started and Jim Fergusson and a few other club members made a terrific name for we Canadians and the B.E.M.C. down there.

Possible the biggest effort for our club was

Tony Miller's spectacular ride in 1938 when he was almost eleven miles in the lead to meet with his disastrous accident.

As we neared the war years quite a few of us were Saturday night soldiers in the Governor General's House Guards, providing our own machines in the despatch riding department. At the time of mobilisation I had been transferred to London, Ontario by my company and so missed the chance to go 'active' with our gang and a bunch from the Falcon Club. G.G.H.Q's were supposed to be a 'reccy' regiment but they were double-crossed by the powers that be, and they finished up in Sherman tanks and did a grand job through Italy ending up in Holland and Germany.

The club carried on in a minor way up to 1940 and we ran the last event at Wasaga in 1937. It was that year that Earl Robinson of Detroit on a Harley Davidson did 109 m.p.h. to set a new Canadian record.

1940 was the end for a while for us and I would like to thank Mrs Marcelle Miller for carrying on the club single-handed while the boys were doing their stuff. She polished all the pots and left them in wonderful shape, handled all the correspondence and the few meagre finances we had and also kept the ACU alive, which we were representing in this country.

In 1946 while at the Falcon Club trial I was approached by an ex-member to re-organise the club and so I ran an ad in the paper that this was our object. We were surprised at the result and held our first meeting in Jim Ferguson's showroom at Scarborough Beach Garage. Jeremy Bankin son of one of our finest Presidents was our first Secretary and Jack Fisher took on the job of guarding the treasury and we were away again. To me fell the honour of being the first post-war President and we went to work with the same ambitions as before.

Running the Castrol and Shell trials and Wasaga Beach were some of our more important ambitions. We were a little fed up about the beach conditions and so we looked around for better stuff. This time we were lucky and managed to get Edenvale Airport. I believe we were the first club in all North America to start this type of racing and I'm afraid that our club was 'IT' in this instance. Around this time a few ex-motorcycle types came around with cars and joined us. Of course our old friend Fergie had always been around and he helped fire the enthusiasm for sports cars that are now the majority of the club. The movement was slow at the start but Doug Cramp, Jack Gillies, Bob Evis and a few others did a large job and the present size of the club is due to their efforts, they've been grand years to me and my interest and enthusiasm is just as great as in 1928.

Extract from 'Small Torque' The magazine of the British Empire Motor Club, August 1957

The British Empire Motor Club is still one of Canada's premier motorsport clubs, and runs motorcycle and car events throughout Ontario. In 2008 the club was inducted into the Canadian Motorcycle Hall of Fame.

Bryan Sparks (H.R.D.) at Wasaga Beach, 1937. This TT Model is believed to be the only H.R.D. that was exported to Canada before WWII. In 1939 he finished fourth at Daytona.

Wasaga Beach by Gerald Barker

Wasaga - what a strange name! To most people in Southern Ontario, it is a familiar name of Indian origin and synonymous with a popular Georgian Bay holiday resort. But to motorcyclists, especially prewar ones, the name carries a very different meaning. Its mere mention to them conjures up thoughts of the past. In their minds, they see a broad expanse of hard packed sand, listen to the roar of well tuned motors, sniff the tang of Castrol R and relive again the racing exploits of such stars as Tony Miller, Earl Robinson, Tommy Neelands, and the late Bryan Sparks.

Wasaga Beach, as a venue for motorcycle racing, dates back fifteen years. The annual sand races organized by the British Empire Motor Club were an outgrowth of the Ontario Tourist Trophy races, which were held at Bayview Heights near Toronto in September of 1932 and 1933. Kaye Don, the well known British automobile racing driver donated a trophy for this event. The magnificent award, which now bears its donor's name, was presented the first year to Edward Hughes of Toronto. Riding a very standard 349cc Rudge, he won the Junior class and established fastest time of the day at 60.02 mph. The following year, this same Eddie Hughes journeyed to the Isle of Man, where he represented Canada in the Lightweight TT, riding a Sunbeam. In 1933, Herb Blair of Montreal, mounted on a 349cc TT Rudge, completely dominated the race meet winning as well as the Kaye Don Trophy, the Junior and Senior

class awards. His average speed for the 77 mile course was 60.01 mph.

The Bayview course was not available in 1934 and as no other locale could be found, races were not held. The search for a suitable course was continued in the next year and it was Vic Fox, one of the members of the BEMC who conceived the idea of using Wasaga Beach for racing. As a native of Barrie, and an aviator who had assisted the Mollisons when they used Wasaga for the take-off on their west to East Atlantic flight, Vic knew the potentialities of the Beach for high speeds.

The Provincial Government was petitioned and permission granted in 1935 for closing off the beach and the organization of the first races

Tony Miller (Ariel Red Hunter)

on Thanksgiving Day, October 24th. The appointed day was cold and windy with snow and sleet blowing off the lake. In spite of this, enthusiastic motorcyclists from all over Ontario congregated on the wind-swept strand and were rewarded with a first class display of skill and daring. The entries numbered 17 and included George Pepper, with his famous Manx Norton and Tony Miller riding the Ariel Red Hunter on which he had made such creditable performances at Keene and Langhorne. Incidentally, both these riders had fitted their machines with streamlined fork cowls - Pepper had also partially enclosed the motor and gearbox. M. Goldhart and Les North had 74 cu in Harley Davidsons; Len Duckworth and Jim Rostron were BSA mounted and J. Fergusson and 'Mad' Sale had their hopes in 2 Stevens.

During the morning, before the main event, quarter mile sprints were held. Goldhart led the field with an even 90 mph with Miller and Pepper tied for second place at 88.24 mph. Due to the inclement weather, the committee exercised their right and reduced the length of the feature race from 100 to 60 miles. There was a massed start with dead motors and right from the outset, Miller took the lead. For 22 laps of the 2 mile course, he set the pace and had already lapped all the other competitors when his motor failed - a broken crankpin! After his retirement, the race developed into a two man affair between Goldhart and Pepper. The Harley rider had the slight edge and he crossed the finish line a few yards in front to complete the course in 59 minutes, 29 sec and win the Kaye Don Trophy.

Les North (Harley Davidson) Wasaga Beach

Chapter 5
THE 1932 TRANS-CANADA ADVENTURE

Graham had continued his long-time, long-range courtship with Wynne Browne, a friendship that started before the First World War, continued through his Birmingham and Bolivia years and his early period in Canada. In early 1930 she sailed across the Atlantic from her Douglas home to become Mrs. J. Graham Oates on June 15th, 1930 in Toronto.

In late 1931 Graham sold out his share of Overseas Motors to return to the Island, where Wynne was expecting their first child and they both wanted their offspring - christened Graham to be born a Manx citizen.

Back on his native soil, and after the birth of Graham Jnr, he hatched plans in early 1932 with George Brown, editor of the 'Isle of Man Weekly Times', for another marathon ride across Canada to help promote the sale of British motorcycles. It was not just to be a straight dash across the country, and this time Graham would attempt to ride as close to the Arctic Circle as was possible.

Ariels were again prepared to back his venture with a newly revamped 500 cc single, now bearing the model name Red Hunter for the first time.

Edward Turner, having joined the firm in 1927, became chief designer in 1930. As well as laying plans to make the Square Four, he heavily redesigned the singles, away from the earlier Val Page design. Graham's machine was very standard with the adoption of a pair of optionally available upswept competition exhaust pipes - no more having to saw them off this time! This was coupled to a Swallow sidecar. This Coventry firm started making sidecars in 1922 before branching out to make a world famous motor car - the Jaguar. The firm was run by Bill Lyons - later to become Sir William Lyons. The outfit was christened "Miss Manxland"

Dunlop provided a pair of special 4-inch tyres that were designed to run on a low pressure, helping them to grip the rail. Other sponsors for the trip included Belstaff, Fibrax brake linings, Skefco bearings, Amal carburettor, Lucas electrics, Smiths instruments, Burman gearbox, Lodge plugs, Tecalemit greasing, Shell petrol and, of course, Castrol supplied the lubricant.

Graham did not fancy taking on the 900+ mile bumpy ride on the sleepers this time, so he designed a pair of small flanged jockey wheels that bolted on strips fore and aft of the machine to enable him to ride the rails. The sidecar wheel spindle was mounted on an extendable axle which allowed it to slide sideways to fit the railway gauge.

Another principal sponsor was Rowntrees who supplied him with a veritable mountain of their Motoring Chocolate and other sweetmeats. The trip was not intended to break any records, so the sidecar carried some films made by The Motor Cycle magazine to show to interested motorcycle clubs on the way, together with a letter of introduction from the Auto Cycle Union's secretary, Tom Loughborough, who was no doubt keen to enrol clubs from the Commonwealth.

Sir Claude Hill, the Island's Lieutenant Governor, checks that Graham's papers are all in order before sending him on the second trans-Canada journey. Wynne accompanied Graham for the UK leg in the sidecar

The initial itinerary for the trip involved Graham sailing directly to Hudson Bay, but this plan had to be abandoned when the cargo boat was unable to find a full load to go that far, so he decided to emulate his earlier cross-Canada ride, with a diversion northwards to get to Port Churchill on the southern edge of Hudson Bay. A bonus for Graham if he got that far was that he would get to view the Aurora Borealis - the Northern Lights - which gave its name to his own machine in 1919.

The trip started from Tynwald Hill, the Isle of Man's open air Parliament site at St. Johns, where Graham was given an official send off by the Island's Lieutenant-Governor, Sir Claude Hill on August 1st, 1932. Then he rode a lap of the TT course before catching the Isle of Man

Steam Packet boat to Liverpool. Before sailing to Canada, he took a 2,000 mile tour of Scotland and England, accompanied by Wynne in the chair for this part of the trip, calling on Ariel dealers and also collecting from civil dignitaries letters which he would deliver to similar civic officials across the breadth of Canada. The bike was given a once over at the Ariel works, and when he went to collect the letter from the Mayor of Birmingham, Graham found the Mayor to be Jim Burman, one of the Burman brothers for whom Graham had worked when he arrived from the Island in 1920.

They made a weekend stop at the Ariel Holiday Camp at Pagham, Sussex where he met holidaying Ariel employees.

Graham kept a most meticulous diary of the

Just prior to leaving the Island. Wilf Harding is seated on Graham's outfit, together with some of his Peveril MCC club members

"The Lord Mayor of Birmingham Alderman J B Burman bidding me good luck outside the Town Hall"

trip, and sent weekly reports back to the Isle of Man Weekly Times throughout the trip, so where possible (I will let) Graham's own words describe the trip.

September 2nd. *"Well, today sees the start of this long-planned trip which all fates have seemingly tried to upset, and then at the last minute relented and did their best to help me, and so 8 o'clock this morning saw me rise in the Bradford Hotel, Liverpool, and kiss my hand to the last bed that will house my bones for some months at least."*

He sailed across on the Duchess of Richmond, owned by the Canadian Pacific Steamship Company. Kaye Don had sailed on the same liner when he took his speedboat Miss England II across to take on Gar and George Wood in a series of match races for the Harmsworth Trophy.

September 5th. *"We heard today that Gar Wood had beaten Kaye Don and we are all very dissapointed. However we will hope for better luck in the other races. I wonder who won the Ulster Grand Prix and today I think it is the Manx Grand Prix. I would have liked to have seen either of them, but more pressing business prevents me."*

September 9th. *"It is 11.30, and the sun appears to welcome us to Canada. I am writing this up to the point where the mail is taken off at Gemouski, and we will then take on the pilot to navigate us up the St. Lawrence to Quebec and Montreal.*

My trials will commence with the Customs, etc., tomorrow. This morning we had our first touch of officialdom, when we were paraded before the doctor."

September 10th. Day spent in Montreal meeting government officials, Castrol reps and setting up a film show for the local motorcyclists. He also took the opportunity to make the first of many calls on local Police Departments to try and persuade them that the British machines, either the singles, or the multi cylindered Square Fours would be better for them than the American Harley Davidson, and Indians they currently rode

September 11th. Montreal to Ottawa, held up by Sunday motorists. *"As I passed a car a fellow shouted "Can-es-theshu" - or something which although I am unable to spell it, meant "How are you" in Manx." He pulled up, and signalled me to do the same, which, of course I did. He shook hands, and said he knew all about me from the 'Isle of Man Times'. His name was Keig, from Montreal, and he has a brother of that name who is a fish merchant from Peel."*

This was the first of many contacts that Graham had with Manx emigres. The Manx Association of Canada, having been forewarned of his trip, made him welcome all through the journey. Arriving at Ottawa, he was hosted by the Greyhound Motor Cycle Club.

September 12th. *"Visited Parliament buildings to obtain permit to enter Hudson Bay; also obtained a small tent and a sleeping bag. Headed off along the banks of the Ottawa river en route to Sault Ste Marie (The Soo). Picked up some bad petrol which made the motor run so hot it melted the grease on the rockers. Ran into a swarm of grasshoppers and was forced to wear over-trousers to stop them going up my legs.*

Under low lying forest and bush, the road is just a cutting through these big Canadian forests, which in this locality are game reserves. A flash of fawn and spotted white denotes a deer passing. I saw a lynx with his eyes shining on me like green signal lamps."

The only meal that day was an apple and some

The start of the Canadian leg of the trip. Ottawa River Bridge, looking towards Hull

chocolate. The Rowntrees bars must have taken up a great deal of space in the sidecar, as on many days it was his staple diet.

September 13th - 14th. Graham stopped at Mattawa for breakfast at a Chinese cafe but the owner seemed more occupied with a body that had been dragged from the river than serving our traveller. Bad roads hindered his progress, and over 50 miles were covered in just first and second gears, so Graham was forced to ride through the night, finally making the Soo at 3.00 am, 500 miles from Ottawa. He slept that night on the floor of the Police Station

"They were very nice to me, I think I will adopt this practice in future. I close my eyes, but the roads continue to dash at me. Fingers swollen, eyes filled with gravel, muscles and back sore. But I have arrived at the Soo and will have a rest tomorrow."

September 14th. Sailed on the Canadian Steamship Liner 'Harmonic' from the Soo across Lake Superior to Port Arthur - now renamed Thunder Bay.

"This boat is a veritable sea-going palace. The accommodation is arranged with the object of carrying the greatest number of passengers and yet providing comfort. I wish there were boats similar to this on the Isle of Man service".

That boat trip took but a single day. The same trip via the railway in 1928 had probably taken Graham several weeks!

September 15th. Disembarked at Port Arthur, met the Mayor at Fort William then drove down Lake Superior to Duluth in the United States. As ever Graham was well prepared for self sufficiency with his fishing gear and rifle.

"It is now eight in the evening and I have just had a meal of lake trout and will move off again towards Winnipeg which is 500 miles away. The night was so bitterly cold that I slept in my sleeping bag fully clothed until 6.00 am when I packed the gear away and set off. By 10 p.m. I was at Winnipeg, having ridden the 501 miles with just chocolate snacks to sustain me."

September 16th/ 17th. Rest and recuperation days at Winnipeg were taken up with the usual rounds of civic, police, and motorcycling functions.

September 18th. As if the trans-Canada trip was not enough, this day saw him competing in the Manitoba Club's long-distance trial.

"Started officially as No. 21 in Manitoba cycle trial at 6.30. Had a little boy as my passenger, the brother of another competitor. The route was by way of Kinova, on the recently-constructed highway from the Ontario boundary. Now in Manitoba. Writing this in a wayside cafe, and the inevitable radio is grinding out music. I will soon be rid of this now, as every mile I go carries me further away from civilization. Well, the run to Kinova was terrible - 300 miles in pouring rain, roads in many places under water, but still my little bike plugged on though it without any trouble. I was compelled to ride for the last hundred miles without glasses or goggles, owing to the rain and mud. I was, however, one of four to finish."

The Manitoba Club is one of the oldest in Canada. As early as 1914 they were holding a Boxing Day Run, which in Winnipeg is saying something because it is usually -20 degrees F with several feet of snow on the roads at that time of year.

September 19th. *"Day spent preparing clothes, obtaining ammunition supplies, peanuts and introduction to people in the North Country."*

September 20th. *"Left at 12 o'clock. Roads gravel and gumbo. Very cold. Everything not well today; the engine is not going well and I am at a loss to understand why. Noticed a large eagle today, and he was fairly close to me. As soon as darkness arrived I had to put on all the clothes I had. I got on the wrong road tonight in the dark and went 40 miles off my route. Spent hours digging out mud from inside the mudguard, the tyre was smoking at one time when rubbing on the packed mud. I will feel more able to deal with it in daylight. To keep warm, or an excuse for being so, I have to dress up to such an extent that I can't see sideways, because if I turn my head, the icy wind seems to get into my bones."*

September 21st. *"I feel that I could just pack up this run if I had the slightest excuse. Had a piece of steel made to help with the mudguard clearing. Horses here have never seen a motor bike, and they try to climb the nearest hedge on my approach. Petrol now 40 cents a gallon which breaks my heart and limited purse. Met the Mayor of Yorkton and newspaper men came after me while I was eating."*

September 22nd. *"The anniversary of the day I arrived in Vancouver after having crossed the Dominion of Canada (1928), and what a birthday today is proving to be. I left for Canora from Yorkton and the morning was glorious, I did not even have to wear my helmet, but how soon the change was to take place. In Canora - first Canadian Northern Railway name for town in 1904, derived from first two letters in each word - I was treated to a glorious sight of mud, mud, mud, for miles and miles. I made a brave effort to succeed, mile after mile in bottom gear, plunging and skidding from side to side. Every few yards I had to clean the mud from beneath the mudguards; eventually I had to take them off completely. I gave in after being exhausted from my efforts at dragging the machine from hole to hole. I then dragged it around, facing where I had started from. I then got a pull with a team of horses, and thence to Canora. I have suffered my first defeat, and here I am back in Canora, staying with a Mr. Crosthwaite who has associations with Ballasalla. Also met a Mr. T. Kennaugh from Ballasalla. In fact I am* wondering what place on earth does not boast of a Manxman."

September 23rd. *"I am waiting for the roads to dry after these terrible rains which put paid to all methods of transport. All being well I should get away for The Pas tomorrow, but I do not like the delay. Well, we will see. Good night. Oates signing off."*

September 24th. *"I have not received the necessary permission to travel to The Pas. I am hoping that I will be ready to proceed tomorrow to cover the remaining part of the road now that the mud has dried up. What a difference a day makes! Today I went through without any trouble. I hope to reach The Pas tomorrow; getting nearer the end of my long run now. My mileage is 4,700. Off early in the morning, so must close.*

At that time north from Winnipeg to The Pas without going far to the west and into Saskatchewan. Winnipeg to The Pas is like Land's End to John O'Groats in distance but over roads scarcely better than a farm lane."

September 25th. *"What a day has passed! I am writing this whilst just trembling with fatigue in a little shack in the bush where I have put up for the night. Covered with mud from head to foot, a sprained thumb and a cut hand, also my face feeling a bit groggy as the result of a meeting with a tree when the machine almost turned over on a rough trail through the bush, where only rabbits, moose, deer etc. have their homes. But to begin at Canora where I left this morning in great spirits which were soon very much dampened. In the first place the attachments for running on the rails left a lot to be desired, and I had to redesign them as I proceeded. The speed on the lines was regulated by my courage, and I had at all times to be ready in case the machine plunged off the*

"A little gumbo mud which is worse than it looks"

Aurora to Ariel   75   the motorcycling life of J. Graham Oates

rails. This happened on four or five occasions and I had then to ride miles on the sleepers until I came to a place where I could lift the machine back on the rails, once I could not find a place so had to lift it on with the aid of a tree trunk. I took to the road in an effort to improve matters and cut right through the bush - a sportsman's paradise around Kakawa with bear, moose duck, grouse, partridge, rabbits etc. in the vicinity. After all my struggles I stuck solid in a bog which came up to the axles of the machine. I struggled and pulled, but it was useless and so had to admit defeat. It was getting dark, I had to make certain of being on the right path, my Dunlop tyre marks proved a good guide. I got back to a little shack and two boys who worked on the railway offered to go with me. The car boasted one light, the motor had to be revved

hard before this was of any use. We pulled 'Miss Manxland' round and then I started back to the shack for the night. A rest, and I will resume the fight tomorrow."

After riding many hundreds of miles on the rails, Graham found that by slightly steering to the left, the outfit seemed to take right hand curves on the rail line much easier; the trouble was when he put just an ounce too much pressure on the handlebars, he pulled the outfit clean off the rails! He remembered that tip for many years afterwards.

September 26th. *"Left Kakawa about midday having spent most of the morning in clearing the mud off the tyres. The weather is great but it threatened to rain a few times and I suffered heart failure because if it rains I am done for as the machine will not stay on the rails, and it not*

"Taken at Sturgis, Saskatchewan showing where the road ended. I then fitted the machine to enable me to ride on the rails and I covered twelve hundred miles in this manner"

a pleasant experience when the machine runs off, many things happen. We left the rails only twice today. (Evening) It is very cold outside and I have just witnessed the Northern Lights; they are marvellous; it is just like a rainbow of green light across the sky, with straight shafts of brighter light, similar to the rays of a searchlight piercing the darkened upper sky. Add the twinkling stars and the tall dark pine trees in silhouette and you have a frightening but splendid picture. I am getting nearer a little each day to this famous Hudson Bay, and I will not be sorry when I reach it, I could do with a wash and shave but will have to do without."

September 27th. *"I waited until 11 o'clock before starting, I made good time until I was thrown off on one of the curves when my guide wheel struck an obstruction. This riding on a narrow ribbon of steel is very hard on the nervous system, and I prefer to ride 500 miles on the road to 100 on the rail. I arrived at The Pas about 12.30, only half an hour before the train. I am getting to love the great wilderness, with its tough ways. Today I am spending in preparing for the final 500 miles, and it is going to be a tough ride. I saw the Northern Lights again, and heard the howling husky dogs. This place is the most northern town in Canada, and is developed as a result of the mining camps."*

September 28th. *"After breakfast I set about getting my machine ready for the next few hundred miles of unpleasantness. Obtained spare tins of petrol and blocks of wood etc. also a jack for lifting the machine on to the track when she runs off. Left The Pas and made for mileage 42 where I knew I could stay with a few of the Air Force boys who are on fire patrol duty. Arrived at 5.30 p.m. and was warmly welcomed."*

September 29th. *"I am reminded this morning that I am due in Fort Churchill today, but I am unable to travel any faster with safety so must be content to proceed safely. I left the miles behind me in great style and was so confident I tried to do 40, when we darted off the rail. It was an awful experience, however I managed to hold the bike from plunging down the bank. Then the fun started in getting it back on the rail. Now going into country with few birds, but many animals. Had a shot at a buck, but missed; however, could not expect much more with a revolver, and whilst moving. I had the unpleasant experience today of having to ride along in the dark in order to reach mile 185 section hut. It was a weird but unpleasant feeling to be riding along unable to see what was before you, however the fates were kind to me and I reached the store at Thicket Portage."*

September 30th. *"Started at 9.30 and did not proceed far until ran off the track. This was caused by frost on the rails, so had to push the machine over the slippery portions until the sun dried them. Some job! Practically all bird and animal life now left behind and at mile 250 or so we seemed to pass into another world. Behind me was a world of brilliant sunshine and blue sky, ahead lay heavy dark clouds which formed a dark, forbidding ceiling. I do not relish going towards it, it looks like snow and then things would be up for me. A few miles and a terrific wind rose, I thought it would blow me off the track at Landing River where I went over a high bridge. I am getting very tired of the continual strain which staying on the rails imposes, I have now accomplished over 500 miles in this way. Arrived at Gellam at 6.15 p.m. and daylight had disappeared."*

October 1st. *"I have not moved a wheel today other than on a gas car. I did not feel very well because of getting so cold last night on my way* to Gellam, so I stopped here for the day. I got out the fishing tackle and went off with the dispatcher on the Hudson Bay Railway."

October 2nd. *"I am now going to have a little breakfast and see if the track is any more dry when I have finished, I have come too far with success to afford to take chances now, with only 185 miles to Churchill. It is snowing very heavily and it looks as f I am here for the day or perhaps even longer. I covered 30 miles today, had to push it three miles because it would slip off if I ran the motor. I reached a high bridge over the Limehouse River where the gaps were three feet wide, of course it was impossible to get the bike over them and I was not prepared to risk riding the rails over the bridge. I had to drag pieces of wood and place them in position in front of the wheels, then go ahead over one gap and then do the same again as I did in the earlier trip. I had a number of narrow escapes from slipping on the wet boards, there was*

nothing to save me from a 200 foot drop if I should slip. I made a push at the sidecar wheel, it gave so easily that I spun over it, but luckily I grasped the axle or sidecar chassis. After exhausting myself I got stuck again, but was rescued by two section men. I then set off in earnest thinking that surely that would be the end of difficulties for one day. But that was not. At mile 164 the outfit plunged down the embankment. I was not hurt, nor was the bike damaged but it seemed impossible for me to get it back on the track, so I took my rifle and binoculars and set off again for help. I walked about five miles and could see nothing, so I decided to go back to the machine for the night. Collected sticks and lit a big fire, because the icy wind was chilling me through. Of course, by this time night had set in and I was most fully prepared for a night in the open within 100 miles of Hudson Bay. A light appears away in the distance. I wonder if it is a train. No it can't

"At mile 164 the outfit plunged down the embankment"

Aurora to Ariel   78   the motorcycling life of J. Graham Oates

"A little help is worth a lot of pity. Getting on to the tracks again"

be; there are no trains today. It must be the 'Lights' What a sight, and what a stroke of luck! A train. I turn on my headlamp pile up the fire and make frantic signals. They stop and I climb into the caboose and am soon well away for the nearest point where I can find a bed. The conductor takes pity on me being hungry and tired, and soon has some tea and four fried eggs ready. How I gobbled them! They found me a good floor to sleep on. Now for a sleep."

October 3rd. *"Out of bed at 5.30 having slept the night in a railway truck. I went out on a gravel train and the fellows lifted the machine up and put it back on the rail. Then I continued. I don't think I was ever so cold as when I arrived at mileage 412. I had a meal in the cookhouse army style, and had a long pleasant talk with some trappers. Got a couple of moose at last; I have always wanted a head. The night was fine, but terribly cold and the Northern*

Lights were crackling and very weird. Did 50 miles today."

October 4th. *"A heavy frost in the night and there are two inches of ice in the water. I am now on the last hundred mile to Churchill and with luck will be there today. Shot seven ptarmigan today alongside the track, I am not such a bad shot it seems, I got these birds at 100 yards with a .22 rifle, I have given them to the cook, so hope to try them tomorrow. I did over 30 miles in second gear, the motor will not get hot enough to heat the oil and so does not develop its full power. The dry wind sweeps from the south ice-fields to break its fury, I lay over the sidecar at times to try and avoid it. My eyes are feeling bad, my nose was frozen inside, and my ears, even inside two helmets, did not have any feeling.*

My struggles, as far as reaching Hudson Bay is concerned, are at an end, as I reached Fort

Crossing the Kettle Rapid Bridge

October 4th *"My struggles, as far as reaching Hudson Bay is concerned, are at an end.*
as I reached Fort Churchill at 6.30 p.m. today"

Churchill at 6.30 p.m. today. When the huge elevators of Fort Churchill came into sight, I gave an inward cheer to my poor, tired spirits" (Later) "I suppose I have now taken a rubber tyred vehicle farther north than any person in the world, and am the only person to ever reach Hudson Bay on a motor of any description fitted with ordinary tyres. The bike has behaved in a wonderful manner and the makers have a lot to be proud of as have Burman for the gearbox and Dunlop for the tyres, which stood up to weeks of abuse, running them as low as six pounds in order they would press down on the railway line and give better grip. Everything on the machine has been grand, including the sidecar which has had to carry a bigger load than it was ever intended to. I have just put my nose outside to put coal on the fire, and Gee! what an ice loaded wind! The speedometer registers 5,146 miles since I left St. Johns. I am going to bring a bottle of water with me and have it as a keepsake with the other one which I obtained in 1928. I do hope that I will be able to get the horns (antlers) home alright, they will look well adorning a hall or other place." (Their final resting place was over the fireplace of Moose Lodge, Baldrine, Isle of Man. They are still there, even though the house is no longer owned by the Oates family.)

Even though they were expecting him, it must have been a weird and wonderful sight on that grey October day for the 500 inhabitants of Fort Churchill. They firstly heard and then saw a motorcycle and sidecar outfit, possibly the first motorcycle some had seen, arriving out of the dark snow clouds along the railway line, the first vehicle other than a tram to arrive there, the whole outfit crowned with a huge moose head which dwarfed both Graham and the bike!

Graham had entered the Hudson Bay lowland

The bottle of water that Graham collected from the Hudson Bay

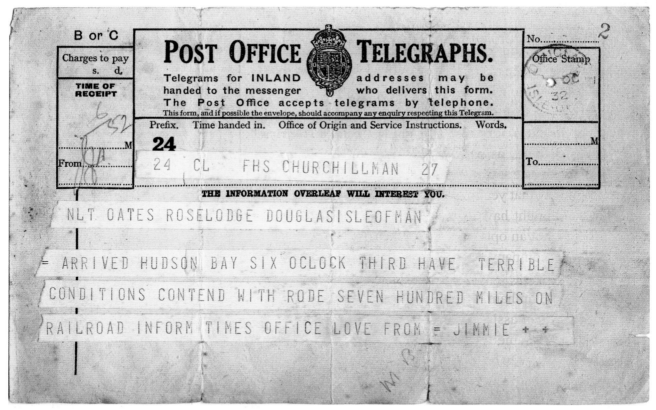

where the climate begins to be influenced by the Arctic waters of the Bay itself, hence the cold and wind. Earlier in the summer it is regular rain and wind. He appears to have cheated being snowed in for the winter by a few weeks at the most.

Graham must have looked quite massive to the inhabitants when he arrived. The reason was that a group of Police who he met on his way to Fort Churchill had donated a fur lined parka for the trip, which was big enough to fit over all his clothing, Belstaff riding coat and all. There was no actual Mayor to hand the letter to in Port Churchill, so George Kydd, resident engineer of the Hudson Bay Railway Terminal was accorded the honour of receiving the mayoral address. His next job was to send a telegram to Wynne and *The Isle of Man Weekly Times*, and then mail the latest instalment of his travelling epistle.

Graham had arranged to have any mail delivered to Churchill. Amongst the letters from home he received a portent of problems back at home in the form of a postcard from 'Gaffer' Littledale, just back from holidaying in Norway. Gaffer, an Ariel riding trials and TT rider wrote *"I do hope you got your money from Ariels before you left, it is very doubtful if they will carry on"* This message from a long-time colleague meant little to Graham at the time, but it was to become crystal clear in a few weeks time.

He spent the next week in and around Fort Churchill, looking at the huge grain elevators and the ruins of the Fort Prince of Wales, built by the Hudson Bay Company around 1700. To Graham the port seemed under utilised, and he advocated its greater use to ship grain further afield. The cargo boats arriving were empty when they could be shipping in Welsh coal at

$7.00 a ton. He had only intended to stay for a day or so, but bad weather delayed his departure. His lodging was the room used by Charles Lindbergh, the aviation pioneer, and his wife, just prior to their flying across the North Pole to Japan in 1930. Graham had to make a concerted decision to move away from Hudson Bay after six days, as the weather reports indicated that the winter storms were approaching early that year, and if he missed his opportunity he might have to stay for the long winter months, not an option he relished.

The railway company arranged to deliver Miss Manxland back to the Hudson Bay Junction, but left Graham to make his own way back. He was given assistance by the locals to stow away on the same train in a grain wagon for the 30-hour journey back to the Hudson Bay Junction. Again his staple diet for that bumpy journey was the inevitable chocolate bars plus some nuts. Retrieving the outfit, he retraced his rail-steps back to Canora, where he fixed up the sidecar wheel on to the original chassis to make it narrower. His rail-riding efforts were at an end, and it was to be roads - or more likely tracks all the way from now on in.

After a day's rest at Canora he travelled westwards, meeting and greeting Mayors, motorcyclists and Police transport officials. The roads were a mixture of gumbo mud, dust, ridges, hollows mixed with the occasional paved highway. The route took him through Regina, Moose Jaw, Medicine Hat, Calgary, Banff, Marble Canyon, and Cranbrook. It was nearing Cranbrook that the sidecar connections started to fail and it was only with assistance from a motorist who carried the cargo from the sidecar that Graham made the town to effect necessary repairs. Punctures also slowed him on this leg of the trip. One time he found the tin of

repair solution had gone missing so he had to soften the solution on a patch with petrol to make it stick to the tube, - it worked too!

Reaching Vancouver, he broke his journey for five days to give man and machine a well earned break. By now the mileage had increased to 7,021 since leaving Tynwald Hill on August 1st. Miss Manxland was left in the care of the Ariel dealer Harry Routledge of Howe Street, Vancouver who gave the valves a gentle grind in and gave the whole bike a general check over. Graham renewed many acquaintances from those years ago including the British Columbia Motor Cycle Club, where he was guest of honour at a dinner. Another welcome reunion was with Charles Dennis Browne, his war time friend, and Castrol man, whose quest for an advertising stunt led to the first trans-Canada trip. Fred Deeley, one of Vancouver's main motorcycle dealers, supplied and fitted Miss Manxland with a screen and handlebar muffs for the return journey.

Another night he went to meet the assembled ranks of the Vancouver Manx Society who stood and sang 'Ellan Vannin' as he entered the room. He collected many letters to deliver back to their relatives in the homeland. The Mayor he delivered the letter to from the Mayor of Manchester was the very same who, four years earlier, had accompanied him to the beach at English Bay to baptise 'Toby', his 1928 outfit with Pacific water, - Louis D. Taylor.

October 30th *Don't know the date but think it is the 30th. However at last I have left Vancouver, I was sorry to leave many good friends behind. On the way from Deeley's store I ran out of petrol and ran into a puncture in the sidecar wheel, so this delayed me a great deal. One of the boys of the B.M.C.C. acted as my escort to the Vancouver Hotel and I said*

Graham with Fred Deeley's at his shop, 915 West Broadway, Vancouver

goodbye to Captain C. D. Browne.

When he entered America at Eastport, Idaho, he covered up the 'Buy Empire Goods' sign he had displayed those many thousands of miles on the sidecar. The roads were wet, but so much better in the States that he was able to ride from Eastport via Wenatchee, Seattle, Stevens Pass, Everett, and back into Canada through Blame, Washington. At the customs he found that he had traversed that corner of America in 23 hours.

October 31st *I am going off down south in order to be able to take a highway which will be passable. I was strongly advised against going back through Canada owing to snow which is now blocking all means of transport from Vancouver to Winnipeg. So I have decided to enter Canada at Windsor and continue my delivery of letters.*

The Lucas lighting set gave a great deal of trouble - *"It is about time that British*

manufacturers produced a lighting set that is capable of giving a little service. Each trip I take, I seem fated to have trouble with electrical parts." He also collected more than a few punctures - the Dunlop covers must have been wearing a shade thin at this time. But not every puncture was caused by the thinning rubber.

"Had lunch at Bellingham, and then I went away alone. Rain started, and it has poured in torrents ever since three o'clock, and I am writing this at ten, whilst waiting for a well-done steak. I feel that I have earned it, for have I not just finished a wrestling match with a burst front tyre which occurred thus; I am at rather a disadvantage when it rains, owing to wearing glasses. When cars are approaching me with bright headlights, I can only see with difficulty between the drops on the glasses. I was skipping along thus tonight, when I struck an iron safety zone stand which was about nine inches high. What a fall I got! And the tyre went 'bang' so I

had the doubtful pleasure of changing the air in the tube."

November 3rd *As I passed village after village I remember certain places where I had experiences of when crossing in 1928. I think my bump of humour must have developed since I left home, as I passed one place today, I burst out laughing aloud. It struck me funny bit I could see myself at a wee store buying yards and yards of rope. This I wound around and around the sidecar tyre in order to protect the tube which was doing its best to climb out of the cover through a hole that had worn. In another I passed where I had to build a wheel from American parts in order to be able to fit a tyre that could be obtained, it being impossible to purchase a well-base English cover.*

It is possible that Graham's monocular outlook would have contributed to the various accounts of his literally 'running out of road', or clipping a corner too close due to the loss of the ability to perceive distances accurately.

The return trip back took him in a mad dash through some of the most scenic areas of the States, but Graham was more concerned with reaching Canada than sightseeing, as winter was breaking early that year. The journey took in part of the route he used 4 years previous, and he remembered some of the towns he visited on that earlier trip. This time the journey was not halted to strip down the engine, nor the ignominy of being towed over the Rockies at Laramie. The '32 Ariel fairly flew over the

```
              INVITATION

          MOTORCYCLE FILMS

      Brought out by Mr. J. Graham Oates.

   You are invited to attend a showing of "The Motor-
   cycle" films produced in England, including:

       The T.T. Race        6 days Scottish Trials
       Colmore Cup          Hill climbing
       Holidaying with a Sidecar Outfit
       The Making of a Motorcycle

   Colonial Theatre, Friday, Nov. 18, 1932, 11 P.M.
   Admission free                  Bring your friends

          Compliments of Fred Deeley Ltd.
```

Escort of the British Motorcycle Club, Vancouver seeing me off for home

mountain range this time.

When he left Rawlins, Colorado, his main intention was to drive himself on to Detroit, Michigan, 1800 miles distance. He failed in this mammoth test of endurance when he stopped at an Indian dealer at Chicago Heights, Illinois, and fell asleep in the showroom. Up to that time he had ridden over 1600 miles in 56 hours, with brief stops for coffee and caffeine tablets to sustain him.

As he returned to Canadian soil he took the cover off the 'Buy Empire Goods' signs on the sidecar and carried on through to London, Ontario where he spent the night, before heading off to Toronto. He was given a hero's welcome by two of his sponsors, Castrol and Rowntrees, and Miss Manxland was put on display at T. Eaton of Yonge Street, the Dominion's largest store, together with a display of Castrol products.

The original intention was to ride on through to Halifax, Nova Scotia, but circumstances across the Ocean made his return a lot different from the triumphant passage he had hoped for.

Whilst Graham was trekking back across America, he was unaware of the troubled affairs of Ariel Motors Ltd., his main sponsors.

The pioneer Birmingham motorcycle manufacturer had built very popular machines from 1902, with a range to cover all sides of the market but, despite this, the 30's recession caught them short of capital and the Selly Oak firm had been bought out by Jack Sangster, formerly the company secretary. It was by all accounts a peaceful takeover, the stock records held by the Ariel Owners' Club show barely any disruption in production when the changeover period came about.

Mr. Sangster did not feel any commitment to honour the obligation shown by Components

Ltd., Ariel's previous owners, so Graham was left on the wrong side of the ocean without the capital to pay for the return leg of his trip! He decided to make for Montreal and see if he could arrange a trip home.

The 'bush telegraph' had been in action since Graham had received the bad news and left Toronto, and a rescue fund was started in the Island by George Brown of the Isle of Man Weekly Times. When he arrived in Montreal two days later he found that members of the Montreal Manx Association with connections in shipping circles had arranged for Graham to work his ticket on the journey home.

The Airthria, a 4,000 ton cargo vessel, was due to sail the next day to Glasgow, but as it did not have any facilities for passengers he was required to sign on as an assistant steward for the trip, at the rate of 1 shilling per month. The vessel, a First War reparation payment from Germany, creaked its way across the sea at a heady 12 knots on a good day. His trip was not made any easier when half the crew, including the captain, went sick with flu just two days into the voyage, and when the stokers succumbed to the influenza later on it slowed the rate of progress down to 8 knots, - cooks don't make good stokers! Graham spent a large part of this seafaring time either peeling mountains of the 'Irishman's friend' - potatoes, or peeling old paintwork and applying fresh coats.

The Airthria was later to be renamed Scapa Flow and was torpedoed by German submarine U413 in 1942.

The cold, grey Scottish December morning must have seemed like paradise to Graham when the rust-bucket finally docked at Glasgow and he could then get back on Miss Manxland, which had been sealed in the hold for the entire 13 day trip.

The trip was still not over yet, as before returning to the Island, Graham had to return to the municipal centres to convey the replies that he collected from the Canadian dignitaries he met on the trip. He visited Edinburgh, Newcastle, York, Sheffield, and then Birmingham, where he received an official welcome from Edward Turner, designer of his machine, at Ariel Motors (J.S.) Ltd., They were obviously keen to get as much publicity from the run, despite their uncaring attitude to honouring the commitment of the former company. The Service Department gave the machine a full inspection after its gruelling

12,000 miles trip and found wear throughout the machine was minimal, and even the original tyres and spark plug were in the machine at the end of the trip.

Further civic visits throughout England were undertaken before Graham finally boarded the Isle of Man Steam Packet vessel Rushen Castle on December 7th, 1932 for the final leg of his long journey. It was a rough crossing, but by this time Graham was well equipped with his sea legs after the Atlantic crossing and was looking forward to some rest and recuperation after one of the longest trips ever made by motorcycle. The Douglas dockside welcoming

Graham's reception at Ariel's on the completion of the trip. The designer of the Red Hunter,
Edward Turner is second from left

party consisted of Wynne and other members of his family, the main dignitaries of the Island, as well as a large contingent of motor cyclists who had gathered that Saturday afternoon to welcome back the man who had put the Isle of Man on the world map. After the quayside welcome Graham fired up Miss Manxland for the last time on the trip and - with all parties in tow - rode the 7 miles to Tynwald Hill to officially sign off the trip that had started 3 months and nearly 13,000 miles previously.

This trip and the 1928 one may seem at this distance in time to be quite similar, but the circumstances behind them were totally different.

Graham first travelled across Canada in 'the Roaring 20's, a time of great economic boom, growth and optimism. The 1932 trip was in the depth of the Depression -'the Dirty 30's' it was called, a time of soup kitchens, massive unemployment and pessimism. And yet on the latter trip he met many people who made an impression on him and on whom he made a considerable impression. The world might have gone to hell in a hand basket in the economic sense, but that did not stop the idealists like Graham Oates.

At the July, 1932, Imperial Conference in Ottawa, Britain gave free access to Empire agricultural products in return for free access for British manufactured goods to the Empire. With the 1931 collapse of the Canadian dollar against the US dollar, US motorcycles had become 20% more expensive. The removal of the tariff against British motorcycles stimulated the import to Canada of many British motorcycles from 1933 onward to 1976.

Many Ariels, singles and multis, were supplied to the Canadian Mounted Police on the back of Graham's endurance effort.

In early 1933 Graham fixed a large wooden three legs of Man symbol to the sidecar and

Graham is greeted by Phil Pike of Pike's of Plymouth; Miss Manxland carries the wooden three legs of Man on her sidecar

undertook a 4,000 mile round-England trip with Miss Manxland to publicise the Isle of Man as a holiday resort, as well as promoting Ariel motorcycles. Whether the Island's Tourist Board realised that Graham had added this last aim to the trip was never made clear. All the major British towns were visited, together with major sporting venues, Brooklands, the Derby, etc. The trans-Canada trip had been well covered by the British national press, so it not surprising that Graham attracted a crowd wherever he went, and more than once he was asked to move on by the Police as the crowds

attending him were causing an obstruction.

Graham was by now a national motorcycle celebrity, often in demand to make personal appearances. He rode from the Island to Hull to act as starter for the Jordan Reliability Trial, organised by motorcycle dealers Messrs Jordan & Co (Hull). This 71-mile event was of a light sporting nature over chiefly secondary roads, and many entrants carried pillion passengers.

But even before the reflections of this memorable trip had a chance to become even recent history, his mind was already busy on yet another project.

Graham with competitors and officials at the Jordan Reliability Trial, June 1933

Chapter 6

RIDING IN THE ISDT AND OTHER TRIALS -
LANDS END TO JOHN O'GROATS ON A SIDEVALVE OUTFIT

Ever since the early 1920s, when he first rode in the ACU Six Days Trial, Graham wanted to ride the International Six Days Trial, which was to be held that year in Wales in 1933. Graham also harboured the notion of running a Manx team and to this end he maintained contacts with the new regime at Ariel's, despite their lack of cooperation in the trans-Canada venture. He went to see Jack Sangster at Selly Oak looking for three Red Hunters for the event, one fitted with a chair for himself, plus two solos to make up an Isle of Man team. What he came away with was the two solo Red Hunters, but his outfit was to be propelled by an overhead camshaft 600 cc Square Four.

The Square Four, a brilliant design from the fertile brain of Edward Turner, came to the motorcycle market in Autumn 1930 as a 500 cc machine. It was introduced into a market dominated almost totally by the big single cylinder machines; the exception to this rule was the Triumph Speed Twin, another Edward Turner creation. In this market place the Square Four was slow to be accepted by the sporting motorcyclists who were used to the successful single cylinder layout. The 'Squariel was enlarged to 600 cc in 1932.

Ariel's logic behind their offer was that if

The Peveril MC & LCC club's team for the 1933 International, with their works Ariels.
Graham, Hughie Kelly and Wilf Harding

Graham could persuade the outfit to give a good account of itself through the trial it would help gain its spurs in the sporting arena. The idea of the four did not immediately appeal to Graham, but never one to look a gift horse in the mouth he enlisted fellow Peveril MCC member Bill Lockington Marshall as passenger and set about mastering the different techniques of multicylindered trials riding.

Bill, a car-driving member of the Peveril Club, had passengered Graham in local trials and quite took to the idea of being a passenger in the International, even though he had never ridden a motorcycle in his life - and still hasn't. Now 88, Bill remembers that the 'Squariel was a totally different animal to ride off-road than the normal single, but it did not take Graham long to master the knack of getting the best out of it, - the four needing to be 'buzzed' through the rough stuff where you would use the torque on a single.

Graham's team mates for the International were a pair of riders whose pedigree was equal, if not better in the field of competitive motorcycling to his own. Hugh Kelly was undoubtedly the outstanding trials rider on the Island in the 30s, winner of countless trials and unofficial Manx trials champion for many years, and Wilf Harding was an all rounder with a second place in the 1930 Junior Manx Grand Prix to his credit - in his first ever road race.

The Manx trio were unable to enter as a national team, as the Island's motorcycle interests were represented by the Auto Cycle Union, but they represented the Peveril Motorcycle and Light Car Club - and the Island, unofficially - in the Club Team Trophy.

The Peveril Club was founded in 1923 and celebrated its 70th anniversary in 1993. It is now primarily an off-road club, concentrating on trials and scrambles, together with the occasional sand race held on the Island's many sandy shores.

When the Peveril's Gill Shield Cup trial was held at Easter of '33, the club was visited by a couple who showed the same pioneering spirit and determination as shown by Graham. They had chosen the Island to get away from the hurly burly of being media personalities wherever they went.

Amy Mollison was the first to arrive in her Moth 'Jason 4', first touching down on Hall Caine Aerodrome, Andreas, then making her way to Ronaldsway. As Amy Johnson, she had proved herself an aviator without peer, pushing aviation boundaries further than ever before, in an era when very few women were making those sort of headlines.

Husband Jim Mollinson, a record-breaking pilot in his own right, later arrived in 'Desert Cloud', Amy's famous Cape record breaking

Jim and Amy Mollison at Glen Helen

machine. Aviation was still in its infancy on the Island in this period, the only map they used to find their way to the Island was barely better than a road atlas, with the Island tucked in the corner. When they left England on their getaway-from-it all trip, they were undecided whether to stop at the Island or head on for Ireland. Jim Mollison was a rather taciturn character, and refused to give any interviews, but they accepted an invitation to have lunch with the Island's Lieutenant-Governor. Their only other engagement was to act as starter for the Gill Shield trial at Glen Helen. A tree planted by Amy still grows in the entrance to the glen.

It is recalled by Graham's brother in-law Bill Penny that the team did not have a strict training regime before the event as all concerned rode competitively throughout the year. Training consisted mainly of arm wrestling, Graham always insisted that it was arm strength, not size or bulk that was needed to master a sidecar. His quite diminutive frame belied his strength of muscle and character.

The 15th International Six Days Trial was based that year in Llandrindod Wells and featured all the classic Welsh hills of yesteryear, Dinas Rock, Bwlch-y-Groes, and Alt-y-Bady amongst six days of high speed off-road riding designed to tax both man and machine to the limit. The Manx team rode down from the island, with the solo machines resplendent in Post Office Red with small Manx flags attached to the handlebars. Graham's outfit had the alternative black finish.

At the weigh-in there was the usual 'horse trading' between trade suppliers, anxious to get as many riders as possible signed up to use their products, be they tyres, chains, oil or fuel. To be able to list as many award winners in adverts was the main reason all the firms were so keen to have the riders using their products. One such rep who befriended the Manx lads was trying to tout for business with a tyre sealant, without much success. There was very little interest in this newfangled product but the Manx lads were persuaded to take the offer of a free 'dose' of the sealant in each wheel just to get the chap off their backs; little did Graham know how valuable this 'free offer' was to be later in the trial.

The Manx team effort failed on the very first day of the trial. Hugh Kelly started well, keeping to the tight time schedule through many checks. Then, later in the afternoon, he had a succession of rear wheel punctures which culminated in the rear wheel collapsing and he was out of the trial, debiting the Manx team with a 100 point loss for each day. Obviously the magic tyre sealant did not do its work for Hugh

Hughie Kelly on his ill-fated first day

Both Graham and Wilf Harding kept their clean sheets right through the trial. Wilf appeared to have had a trouble-free run all week, but Bill recalls that he and Graham had a fairly eventful event with the outfit, no more so than on the fifth day of the trial when Graham tipped it upside down! The tool kit was housed under the seat of the sidecar, but this liberated itself out through the well-battered bottom of the sidecar body after a few days. As the rules did not allow any outside assistance, this included tools etc., replacement spanners were 'found' and stowed away in a more secure position.

During Wednesday, the whole trial almost came to a grinding halt at Dinas Rock, near Penderyn. The loose shaley surface was almost impossible to climb, and if anyone stopped it caused utter chaos for those following, with failed riders either turning round to have another attempt, or just simply sliding backwards down. Outside assistance was - theoretically - not allowed, and Graham instructed Bill to 'desist' anyone from trying to help, for fear of exclusion. In the midst of the chaos at Dinas Rock that day, was a gentleman standing by the side of their outfit shouting "clear the course, clear the course". Graham's comment, when he gave a talk on his experiences in 1963 was "It would have taken a

The chaos that was Dinas Rock. Graham (No. 9) waits for a clear path behind A. G. Mapstone (750 Zenith, 14) who overturned the outfit later that day. Bill Marshall is in conversation with Tom Loughborough, Secretary of the ACU. No. 7 is Gold medal winner H. J. Finden (495 A.J.S.) and No. 10 is Stuart Waycott (348 Velocette) who retired

Follow the leader: George Goodall (997 Morgan), later to be MD at Morgan, is followed by a travelling marshal, Graham (9) is followed by A. Vitvar (74 Jawa)

bloody helicopter to clear that damned hill"! Graham later found out that the person doing the shouting, and whom Bill very nearly forcibly tried to 'desist' from helping the outfit up Dinas Rock was Tom Loughborough, Secretary General of the Auto Cycle Union, who was in fact trying to keep the trial moving. Later that day Bill had the feeling something was wrong, when suddenly he was feet-up and facing the sky, - the bolt holding the sidecar nose to its suspension spring had pulled through the light alloy sidecar body. A jacket belt was pressed into action to hold the nose in position for the rest of the day and repairs were made good before the final speed test, held at Donington Park.

With his racing experience, and revelling in racing on a purpose built track for the first time, Will Harding led the final speed test for the solo 500s at Donington from start to finish. Fellow

Peveril club members Harold and Bertie Rowell, both Manx Grand Prix leaderboard men, had travelled across as backup support crew for the Manx team. The pair of them were frantically signalling Wilf to slow down in the speed test, fearful that he might blow the engine and lose his Gold.

Just prior to the sidecars taking their turn on the track for the speed test, Bill noticed a large nail in the front tyre. Their dilemma was - had it punctured the tube, and if so - did they remove the nail and risk having a flat - or leave it in and risk sudden tyre failure at high speed. Graham opted to pull the nail, and after a couple of seconds of air escaping, the tyre sealant - fitted but forgotten about - did its work and sealed the hole. In the early days it was not unusual to run the whole trial on the same set of tyres, but these days the riders change tyres most days. Graham was by then thoroughly attuned to

The final speed test at Donington. Bill Marshall is barely visible behind Graham as they prepare to lap Harry Perry (645 Triumph). Perry won the Maudes Trophy with the same outfit later in the year, covering 500 miles in 500 minutes round Brooklands. No. 83 is G. J. Spooner (348 Ariel)

riding the four, and gave it full noise in the speed test. With Bill alternately flinging himself out over the sidecar mudguard and over the back wheel, the pair clocked up more laps than any other outfit round Donington to claim a well deserved Gold Medal, - one of 56 Golds gained from an entry of 140.

At the conclusion of the event, the riders were invited to Nottingham University for the prize giving. Graham had promised Bill his Gold medal, but when he went up to claim it he returned empty handed, Ariel Motors (J.S.) Ltd. had nabbed it for their trophy cabinet, one of the penalties of being a works rider. As Wilf Harding was loaned his Red Hunter, he was allowed to retain his 'gong'. His widow has it mounted on a gold chain, and it is a treasured possession within the Harding family.

Just after the International, with the organisers' seals still intact on the outfit, Graham and Bill made a successful attack on Snaefell via the railway lines, using the same method of bridging the culverts that Graham used at the Montreal Bridge in 1928, they carried two small planks for the purpose. The trip was filmed by one of the newsreel companies, but this film has not yet been traced. This was Graham's only three-wheeled attempt on Snaefell; this was first conquered by Tommy Corlett - sole survivor of the Aurora workforce - on his Ixion outfit just after the first world war.

That winter the Manx team were honoured at the Island's ACU dinner, where Bill Marshall was presented with a gold medal, bought for him by his team mates in recognition of his exploits in what was to be his only International Six Days Trial. He went on to become one of the Island's premier car rallyists after the event, but still retained fond memories - and the gold medal - of that eventful Welsh trip.

The 1933 Trophy contest was won by a trio of BMW mounted riders from Germany, with the victors opting to run the event in 1934.

Wilf Harding never again rode the International Six Days Trial, but Hugh Kelly's International career spanned 29 years. He never managed to win the elusive Gold medal, missing it on one occasion because he flagged down some British team members who had gone off route to point out their error. He was scant seconds late at the next check, so bang went his Gold. Hugh always rode Ariel except for his last event. Having retired from competitive riding, he was persuaded to take over Eddie Crooks AJS entry, but the change of mount still did not bring that elusive medal. Hugh's son Roger was to fare much better, as he won a Gold in 1971 on Rolf Tibblin's personal 420 cc Husqvarna when the trial was held on the Isle of Man.

The same team of riders, with fellow Peveril club member Jimmy Newson taking the place of Bill Marshall in Graham's chair, took part in the Scottish Six Days Trial in May, 1934. Wilf Harding made the best performance of the Manx trio, gaining a silver cup, being among the first 30 per cent of the entry; the others gained gold medals. Hughie Kelly started the trial in fine style, losing no marks to lead after the first day, but gradually slipped down the field. The weather was poor all week, with rain on most days. Jimmy Newson, a star solo rider in his own right, lost his appetite for sidecar passengering after spending most days sitting in a pool of water in the sidecar. To raise funds for the Scottish, the riders arranged a charity soccer match between the Peveril M.C.C. and the Peel Ladies football team. The bikers were soundly thrashed!

The International gold winning performance was not lost on the Ariel factory, and they enrolled Graham for the 1934 I.S.D.T., held in Germany and based around Garmisch Partenkirchen. Mounted this time on a more familiar Red Hunter outfit, again linked to a Swallow sidecar, once more passengered by local tobacconist Jimmy Newson, who must have forgotten his uncomfortable Scottish trial. Once again he captained a Peveril MCC club team; this time his team mates were Fred Vigers and Reg Cotterill, the three of them also nominated as the Ariel 'B' team in the manufacturer's trophy contest.

Passenger Jimmy Newson with their 1934 ISDT and Scottish six Days Trial outfit

The trial was another of strength and stamina, with the BMW mounted German team, which included Ernst Henne, later to hold the motorcycle land speed record, once again being victorious over the British team.

1934 was to prove Ariel's finest International Trial, with both their 'A' team - comprising Len Heath, Jack White, and J.C. Edward, - and Graham's 'B' teams, completing the whole trial without losing a single mark to take first and second places in the Manufacturer's Team competition. The Peveril trio finished third in the Club Team section, again without loss of marks, beaten only on special test times by the Dublin University MCC & LCC team of G.M. Campbell, (346 New Imperial), S. Moran (498 Matchless) and A.H.L. Archer (497 Ariel). Second was the Sunbeam MCC club, Len Heath (497 Ariel), J. White (497 Ariel) and S. Cmyral (248 Puch) the latter team beating the Island trio for second place by just 38 seconds.

Not long after riding the I.S.D.T, Graham made plans for an attempt on the Land's End to John O' Groats. The ACU had banned any record attempts on the open roads many years before; the last official record stood in the name of Ivan B. Hart-Davies, who made the trip in 33 hrs. 22 minutes in 1909 on a single-speed belt-drive Triumph. Even without calling it a 'record attempt' Graham hoped to complete the run in under 24 hours, but instead was persuaded by Jack Sangster, boss of Ariel's, to make the trip with a 557 cc VB side-valve outfit, without stopping the engine throughout the entire trip.

Graham was unconvinced that the side-valve power unit would stand the racket, so, borrowing one from Ariel's, he rode it 800 miles in the National Rally, just to convince himself of its suitability. As expected, Graham won a gold medal in the National, in addition to setting the best performance by an Ariel rider.

The Land's End to John O'Groats run took place in September 1934, when Graham, together with ACU official E. B. Ware, the pre-war Morgan racer, installed in the sidecar, left the Land's End Hotel at 3 a.m. in a squally shower, which had changed to snow by the time they reached Exeter. On they went through Taunton, Clifton, Gloucester and Worcester into Birmingham.

That very day Ariel's were holding a celebration dinner at the Midland Hotel in honour of their successful Six Days Trial riders so Graham made for the Hotel to meet his team mates and grab a quick celebratory glass of

The 1934 Ariel 'B' team of Reg Cotterill, Graham and Fred Vigars at Ariels ISDT celebration dinner. Graham's rather unkempt appearance is explained because he was part way through the sidevalve trip from Land's End to John O'Groats

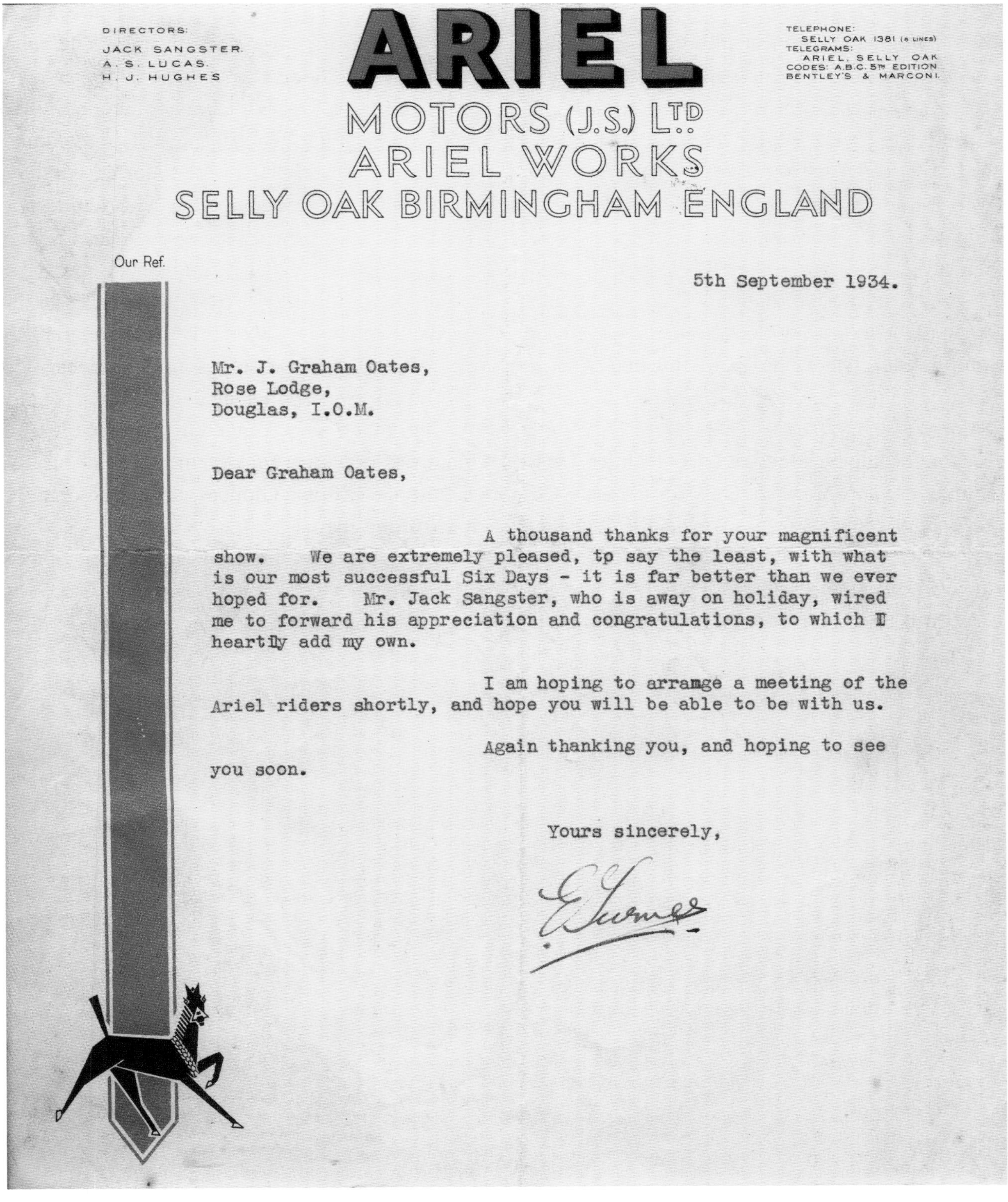

ARIEL
MOTORS (J.S.) LTD
ARIEL WORKS
SELLY OAK BIRMINGHAM ENGLAND

DIRECTORS:
JACK SANGSTER.
A. S. LUCAS.
H. J. HUGHES

TELEPHONE:
SELLY OAK 1381 (5 LINES)
TELEGRAMS:
ARIEL, SELLY OAK
CODES: A.B.C. 5TH EDITION.
BENTLEY'S & MARCONI.

Our Ref.

5th September 1934.

Mr. J. Graham Oates,
Rose Lodge,
Douglas, I.O.M.

Dear Graham Oates,

      A thousand thanks for your magnificent show. We are extremely pleased, to say the least, with what is our most successful Six Days - it is far better than we ever hoped for. Mr. Jack Sangster, who is away on holiday, wired me to forward his appreciation and congratulations, to which I heartily add my own.

      I am hoping to arrange a meeting of the Ariel riders shortly, and hope you will be able to be with us.

      Again thanking you, and hoping to see you soon.

Yours sincerely,

Ariel Motors letter of appreciation of his ISDT success

champagne. The ACU observer was not so lucky however, as he was still ensconced in the sidecar, watching the side-valve motor patiently tick over all the time with the exhaust pipe starting to glow cherry red! Graham did not stay too long at the Hotel before regaining the saddle to head for Whitchurch. On and relentlessly on went the outfit, through Chester, through the then-new Mersey Tunnel to Liverpool and Preston. After Kendal they made a navigational error, turning left to Windermere instead of right for Carlisle. They were faced with the choice of either retracing their steps right back to Kendal or riding over the 1,400 ft. Kirkstone Pass, a formidable enough road to have been included as an observed hill in the 1920's Six Days Trials. Graham chose to tackle the pass and the side-valve chuffed its way to the top with no bother.

In Carlisle Graham had a change of observer. E. B. Ware vacated the sidecar - not altogether unwillingly - and his place was taken by R.A. Prescott, son-in-law of an Island Lieutenant Governor Sir Claude Hill. Just as they entered Scotland the effort - but not the engine - was temporarily halted by an eagle-eyed policeman who spotted that the tail light was not working. It was difficult to explain that they could not stop the engine, and agreed to produce licence, insurance etc. later at Birmingham, which he reluctantly agreed to. The first signs of sleepiness fell over Graham approaching Perth, where he pulled over for a cup of black coffee supplied by his observer, plus the inevitable bar of chocolate, Rowntree's, of course! The weather was still inclement but no further problems were encountered until Blair Atholl, where one of the Duke of Atholl's deer suddenly leapt out of the darkness, careered into the front wheel and vanished as quickly as it came! It must have reminded him of a similar incident during the first world war.

Reliance Trial action, 1934

Do you remember?

ON October 24, 1934, "Motor Cycling" reported a most remarkable run from Land's End to John O'Groats on a 1935 550 c.c. side valve Ariel combination, the engine of which was kept running all the time.

This, of course, is a feat of endurance rarely demanded from any normal touring engine, but it nevertheless demonstrates the ample margin of strength built into all Ariel machines.

When you buy your post-war outfit, remember that Ariel gives you more than you can ever demand.

ARIEL

**ARIEL MOTORS LIMITED
SELLY OAK, BIRMINGHAM**

A wartime Ariel advert extolling the success of Graham's Lands End to John O'Groats run

Aurora to Ariel   101   the motorcycling life of J. Graham Oates

At 10.45 a.m. the outfit rolled to a halt outside the John o' Groats Hotel, the engine still running as it had done so for 31 hours and 45 minutes, during which time they had covered 913 miles. Once more the observer vacated the chair for the comfort of a train journey home, leaving Graham with a solitary ride back to Birmingham.

In 1935, he moved the family across to Liverpool, where he worked for Sergents. He joined the Liverpool Motor Club, another club like the British Empire Motor Club of Canada, with which he held a long association, holding the post of Vice President for a great many years with motor race champion Juan Manuel Fangio and Brooklands record holder and TT rider Victor Horsman.

September 1936 saw Graham once more at Garmisch-Partenkirchen for the International Six Days Trial, once more Red Hunter outfit mounted, passengered by Norman Williams, this time riding as a privateer. It was not to be a successful event, as he retired at the end of the first day after losing 25 marks on time at the last two check points of the day. His retirement defeated any hopes the Liverpool Motor Club had of winning the team prize, but both their other riders, A.C. (Bill) Kelly, (498 Rudge), - not a Manx Kelly - this one was a Liverpudlian - and John E. Wade, (348 Norton), came through the trial with Gold medals.

Action from the 1936 ISDT, held at Garmisch-Partenkirchen

Chapter 7

THE 1939 ISDT - FLEEING GERMANY - SCOOTER AND VINTAGE CLUB RALLIES

Graham had continued to ride one day sporting trials on his faithful Red Hunter as a member of the South Liverpool Club.

After five single-cylinder years, he was again mounted on an Ariel Square Four for the International, which was once again held around Llandrindod Wells, scene of his gold medal performance in 1933. This time the 'Squariel' was the 1,000 cc push rod version, But this 1938 event was one where the Oates luck deserted him. Chassis trouble was the quoted reason for his retirement on the second day, after losing four marks on the first day. The same trouble was also listed as the reason for the retirement of Harold Taylor, the one-legged rider of a similar outfit. This trial was particularly difficult for sidecar competitors. Of the 35 starters, only three were to finish, with only one, W. Reinhardt (597 BMW), maintaining the penalty-free gold standard run.

After working for Ebbs Motors of Walton, Liverpool for many years, Graham took over

An undated shot, with a selection of trophies outside Ebbs Motors

NEARER TO THE ARCTIC CIRCLE ON A MOTOR CYCLE — *THAN ANY OTHER MAN !!*

THIS WAS ACCOMPLISHED BY MR GRAHAM OATES ON AN 'ARIEL' MOTOR CYCLE AND SIDECAR!

"Ebbs" are the kind of people who will do anything to ensure contented customers and incidentally what they, and their staff don't know about "Ariel" motorcycles isn't worth mentioning!

An Ebbs advert

the firm in 1938 and ran it as Graham Oates Motors, selling both bikes and cars. Graham kept himself busy at this period not only with the motor business, but also giving illustrated talks of his riding career, aided by a vast number of slides that he had taken on both of the Canada trips. It was not only to motorcycle clubs that he gave the talks. An excerpt from his scrapbook, taken from a Merseyside newspaper reads: *'On Feb. 23rd (1939), Mr. Graham Oates, the well-known motorcycling globe trotter, will give an address to the inmates of Walton Gaol, Liverpool. The subject will be 'From the Isle of Man to Canada by Motorcycle', but we hope it will not inspire its hearers with a will to wander!'* A note from the Prison Governor after this visit relates that when the chaplain arrived home after the talk he found his house had been burgled!

At this time Graham was promoting the use of autocycles, and to prove his point he rode an HEC in the 1939 National Rally, held in June that year. This was an 80 cc machine fitted with their own two-stroke engine, and they were manufactured in the old Levis factory at Stechford, near Birmingham. Graham managed to clock up 346 miles and 18 checkpoints in the 24 hours with the autocycle, but finished without an award.

Graham's last major event was the 21st International Six days Trial of 1939. Although it was run by Germany, the headquarters were in Salzburg, Austria. He had secured a late entry, as he was unsure of getting a machine, since the Selly Oak works were gearing up to produce bikes for the army. The machine arrived late, and fettling it for the event had taken much

Trials outfit transporter - 1950s style

longer than anticipated, so he had a mad dash to get over to Salzburg for the start of the event. It was only the assistance of a letter from the Secretary General of the FIM that helped him clear the customs into Germany quickly and get to the start on time. As in 1938 his mount was another 1,000 cc Square Four outfit, this time fitted with a sprung wheel Noxal sidecar, one of three such outfits entered in the trial. This cumbersome addition made the outfit a real heavyweight and wide beast, quite unlike the sleek, nimble 600 cc version he had ridden in 1933. The newly built Autobahn was a revelation. It was a great boon to a latecomer, as the Square Four was in its element on such a road, but although it ran perfectly for the run to Salzburg, it was to give trouble right from the start of the event.

The trial had started with Europe under a threat of a German-Russian war, and many riders had withdrawn their entries. An announcement of a Non Aggression pact between the two super powers may have raised the hopes of the home nation that an imminent war was being averted, but most other nationals were of a different opinion. The Germans did not really expect anyone to enter, and were somewhat taken aback when they received the official British entries, plus many privateers. Italy was the only other country to send official Vase and Trophy teams. It was under politically unsettled conditions that Graham and the 60 British riders started the event.

On the first day's run he ran out of petrol high in the mountains, but was able to coast 4 miles down to a checkpoint to refuel. Later, he damaged the rear wheel spindle - and his passenger's nerves - when he was forced to jump the outfit over a hedge into a field to avoid a fallen Italian rider. The heavy outfit was difficult to ride over the byroads and, trying too hard, he went off course in a big way a few times. Once it caused the outfit to be wedged tight between two very substantial trees, and these troubles resulted in his losing 58 marks for the day. In addition there appeared to be problems with the ignition system, so Graham was not too optimistic for his chances on the second day. The next morning the machine failed totally to start from the Parc Ferme where all the competitors' machines had been impounded

Graham's starters medal for the 1939 International, his only souvenir of the event

overnight, and he was forced out of the event. Lack of spark was the reason for the retirement. A group of German bike enthusiasts stripped and rebuilt the magneto that day, after which the machine ran faultlessly, and Graham took to an unaccustomed spectating role.

At the end of the fourth day of the trial there came a telegram from the Home Office ordering all civilian riders to leave the trial and make best haste away to neutral Switzerland. This was particularly galling for the British Silver Vase 'B team who were still without loss of marks, and their Trophy team was only four marks behind the leading German team. But Government orders had to be obeyed, and the motley crew of riders, support crews, and spectators packed their bags and made preparations to head away. Surprisingly, four privateers, - Marjorie Cottle, Hugh Sim, Colin Edge and Alan Saunders - plus Graham - had not received the instructions as their lodgings were well outside the town. Indeed Colin Edge had to hire a bicycle to get him the mile and a half from his hotel to the start of the trial every day. Having missed the exodus they decided to stay on with the Army riders and see the trial out. But the very next day a further telegram from the War Office revealed the deteriorating situation and ordered the Army to abandon, so the final five joined the Army convoy and headed off.

Even though he was out of the trial, Graham had still been collecting his allotted fuel ration for each day and secreting it away in a milk churn, hidden in a bush in the grounds of his hotel. His passenger had left with the rest of the British privateers so there was plenty of room for the churn in the sidecar. The organisers arranged for a Colonel Grimm to escort the riders back to the frontier, and his presence proved invaluable as he was able to force petrol stations to open to refuel the riders and support vehicles. Whenever this happened the streets also filled with locals hoping to get fuel, but they were denied supplies. Lack of sleep was a major problem for the riders, and many fell asleep at the controls. Marjorie Cottle hit a tree when she dozed off, injuring her face. Her bike was put onto a support wagon, which meant that one of the resting Army riders was pitched off to continue the ride home. The German Colonel also came to the rescue when they stopped for a final meal on German soil near the German / Swiss border at Lake Constance. Coffee, jam, and rolls appeared in plentiful supply on the table, but with only two small pats of butter. Grimm disappeared into the kitchen, and when he reappeared, so did a voluminous quantity of butter and hard boiled eggs. The representatives of the two nations wished each other well at the border, and went their separate ways.

There was still a long trek back to Boulogne from Switzerland, and most of the machines were lacking lights by this time. The convoy ran nose to tail with one good headlight at the front and a working tail light at the rear. Although they saw little sign of military activity in Germany, the rest of Europe the convoy sped through was busy making military preparations. The tank traps were already in place and full mobilisation was taking place. Their headlong chase for the French coast was halted in Belgium when they were arrested on suspicion of being German spies and brought before the local Mayor, but the situation was resolved and they carried on to the port.

In France, Graham left the main convoy and headed on alone. By this time, barely a few days before Germany invaded Poland, word of an impending conflict had spread to most of the

British nationals abroad and the roads to the coast were full of British registered cars heading for the safety of home. A great number of the cars were abandoned by the roadside, out of fuel, and when Graham was flagged down by a couple standing by a Rolls Royce, he assumed correctly that they too had run out of petrol. There was still sufficient in the churn to let them replenish their tank without any danger of leaving Graham stranded, so they all set off in Ariel / Rolls Royce convoy to Boulogne. It was only in the safety of the boat as it crossed the English Channel that night that the identity of the rescued couple came to light - they were Hollywood film producer Alexander Korda and his newly wed wife, the actress Merle Oberon, who had been abroad on honeymoon when the

troubles came to a head.

The RAC was in charge of the evacuation, but they refused to put the vehicles on the boat that day, so both were abandoned on the French quayside. Graham was certain he had seen the last of the outfit that day, but it was returned on a cargo boat the next day, and he sped back to Liverpool.

This unrewarding episode was to bring a curtain down on the 20-year long competition career of J. Graham Oates.

The Ariel was never returned to the works as agreed, and it was later to be blown to smithereens by a direct hit on his garage during a German air raid that was targeted on the port of Liverpool. This air raid also ended Graham Oates Motors!

Major J.W. Graham Oates, 9th Training Battalion (D) R.A.S.C. - the oficial photograph

Major J.W. Graham Oates, 9th Training Battalion (D) R.A.S.C. - as depicted in the Battalion magazine

The winning Training Battalion (Drivers) team at a North Midlands Area trial. Left to right: Capt J. Stephens, Cpl G. Garth, Sgt R. Jessopp, 2nd Lt. J. M. Ching, Cpl A. Lockwood, L-cpl D. D. Weaver, Cpl G. Moxon and Graham

As WWII took shape, Graham, now 41, volunteered his services to the Army, an offer which was speedily taken up by the Royal Army Service Corps. The role of the motorcycle despatch rider was to be as vital in this war as the time when Graham himself was riding a model H Triumph between the trenches in WW1. The Army needed to find a core of rider/instructors who could speedily and efficiently train a new breed of despatchers, and there can have been no better role model for the thousands of rookie motorcyclists than someone who had ridden many thousands of miles on the type of machines that they were now to rely on. Indeed that might well be their lifeline. Many of the rider training instructors were competition riders, both on and off-road aces.

Throughout the war period many thousands of

riders passed through training camps spread all over Great Britain to be given a thorough grounding in motorcycling - both riding and mechanical. That was to prove as big a springboard for the massive increase in two wheeled sales and awareness when peace time came as that which had happened after the first world war.

Many of those volunteers had never even ridden a motorcycle on the road, let alone across all sorts of terrain, so to assist them in learning the skills of riding, Graham and others initiated a series of trials / tuition courses, with the skills of the cream of the pre-war trials aces being demonstrated over the varying terrain before the volunteers tried their hand.

George Brown, Editor of the Isle of Man Weekly Times, visited one of Graham's training camps in Derbyshire during 1943. He commented on the comradeships between the ranks, the cosy billets and their 'hide-out' - a services only club, and made great mention of a number of murals that decorated the walls. 'We have not seen such picturesque scenes since the last war, when you used to see similar pictures to gladden the hearts of the men in the trenches. No further description of these pictures is possible"

At one demonstration-cum-trial held 'somewhere in England' - probably around the Ripon area of Yorkshire, the instructors included Allan Jefferies, Jack Booker, Jack Williams, Bert Perrigo, George Rowley, Vic Brittain, not forgetting Graham, a veritable "who's who" of Britain's international trials aces. Later in the War Graham was transferred down to the Eastbourne area, where it was not all work, and he spent many a happy day shooting pheasant on fellow Ariel rider Len Heath's South Coast estate along with many fellow officers.

At the end of the war Graham was demobbed - for the last time - but the organisational skills he demonstrated with the rider training camps were still in demand by the British Government.

At the ending of the Second World War, Germany was in ruins, bankrupt economically, financially, and without any credible organisation after the dissolution of the Third Reich. The Control Commission was set up by the Allied Forces whilst they began the reconstruction of their former enemy's infrastructure. Graham was seconded to help the rebuilding of the German road transport system.

Conducting a B.A.O.R. trial, 1946

One person who got to know Graham well at this time was Raymond Baxter, a former fighter pilot who was destined to be the BBC's foremost motor sport reporter. Raymond recalled his days in Germany.

"In the Winter of 1947 I was taken on to the staff of the BBC on a two year contract for immediate secondment to the job of Production Manager and Deputy Station Director of the British Forces Network, Hamburg. With the Station Director, an experienced and charming BBC man called John Humphries, we were the only two British civilians in a staff consisting of British Service personnel still in uniform, and German civilian employees.

Unlike the vast majority of British civilians working in Germany at that time, we were not employed by the Control Commission - the organisation set up effectively to 'run Germany' in the chaos following the collapse of the Third Reich. But, needless to say, we made many friends amongst the CCG community who were, after all, a major part of our BFN audience. Amongst these was Col. Graham Oates, at that time head of the Roads and Road Transport Section of the CCG, responsible for the whole of the British Zone in that context.

Precisely where and how we met I cannot now remember, but we became close friends, despite the disparity in our ages. I was 25; he had served, albeit as a very young man, in the first World War, and achieved the rank of Colonel in the Second. He was every inch the part - ramrod straight, always immaculate, somewhat clipped in speech, unfailingly courteous and charming.

Gradually, over drinks at the famous bars of the Atlantic and Four Seasons Hotels, I came to hear of his amazing achievements on two, three and four wheels during the years between the wars; of his life as a lumber-jack in Northern

Canada, a cowboy in Alberta, of his T.T. racing in the Isle of Man, and his various high-speed and long-distance record attempts.

Despite his modesty, I persuaded him to sit down in front of a microphone in one of our BFN studios, and tell some of his stories - unscripted in those days a highly unconventional method of broadcasting. At BFN we were amongst the first in the world to record on magnetic tape. We had acquired the equipment invented and used by the Germans during the War, and we employed experienced and excellent German technicians to operate it. Consequently I was able to "edit on tape" Graham's material, and we broadcast his reminiscences in a short series of four or six programmes. I think I entitled it "Adventures on Wheels", but I can't be certain.

He also joined me as a fellow commentator in a number of "live" outside broadcasts which I set up. These covered amazing motor-cycling events arranged by the Army: - closed-circuit road racing, scrambles, trials, and (would you believe?) speedway racing on dirt or grass tracks. It was all wonderful fun, organised and competed in by officers and men in uniform, using what machinery was available, the standard despatch rider's WD Nortons, BSAs, Triumphs, and an occasional Velocette, all tuned and modified to the ultimate ounce of power available.

There were separate classes for 'acquired' BMWs and other equipment, including specialist speedway bikes, which could not possibly have appeared in any British Army inventory.

Despite his official status as a civilian, I know that Graham Oates played a major role in the furtherance of these excellent pursuits. Petrol rationing, for example, was a critical factor presenting an obstacle which had to be overcome.

Graham was also responsible for Germany's first post-war motor race meeting. It was held over a course in the Stadt Park in Hamburg - the equivalent of London's Hyde Park - in, I think, the Spring of 1948. Organised officially by the reformed ADAC - Allgemeiner Deutscher Automobil Club - it was a series of sports and touring-car races which could not have been staged without his official sanction and support.

I believe, though I have no documentary evidence to support my recollection, that this was the first appearance of what was to become Porsche. A much modified Volkswagen driven by the son of Ferdinand Porsche won, hands-down.

At that time, Graham had a beautiful white BMW 328, which he thought to have been a "works car" and which he invited me to drive in those races. For some obscure reason, which again I cannot remember, I was unable to accept, to my intense annoyance.

He also bought from the factory in Coventry, and drove back to Hamburg, one of the earliest Triumph 1800 Roadsters - by far the most beautiful model ever produced by the marque and forerunner of the eminently successful TR range.

Another motor-sport enthusiast in Hamburg at that time was Tom Walkerley, brother of Rodney - 'Grande Vitesse' of Motor magazine. Together, with Graham as the driving force, we formed the British Automobile Club Hamburg. Amongst my collection of trophies are two tankards, which I greatly value. They are inscribed "BACH June 1949 - Class Win" and ditto 'Team Award'. The event was a typical silver Club rally of the period, open to any member, regardless of his car, previous experience, whether he was a member of HM Forces or civilian, whether he was the owner of his mount, or whether, within the letter of the law, it was his in which to compete.

Thus we had an assorted 'field" ranging from an ex-Gestapo Horch and a vintage Vauxhall, to a brand-new Hillman Minx, entered by Capt. the Hon. Gerald Lascelles, latterly to become the distinguished and highly successful President of the British Racing Drivers' Club, and a formative figure in the post-war "golden age" of British motor racing.

My own mount was a Standard Eight drophead coupe which, following Graham's example and introduction, I had purchased ex-works, and driven to Germany. Also, thanks to Graham's introduction to "Pen" Penrice, the Triumph PRO, and his side-kick, the unforgettable Jack Croft, the cylinder-head was "a whisker" shaved, and the engine was "subject to works approval".

The course of the rally was the most imaginative which we, as organisers, could conceive. Thanks to the influence of Graham Oates, it incorporated a "cross-country" section on British Army tank-training ground, and a "maximum-speed" section over the yet uncompleted Hamburg-Bremen Autobahn.

It was, by any standards, a good event.

My wife and I continued to maintain contact with Graham after we left Germany and enjoyed the warmth of his friendship until his untimely death."

It was not just the roads that Graham was involved with. Civil engineering had to be restarted in Germany to get the economy back on its feet again, repair the roads and provide employment for their many former soldiers, and this included motor manufacture. The Volkswagen factory was one of the first to get

Raymond Baxter interviews the R.A.S.C. team before the 1948 International Six Days Trial, for the British Forces Network

back into manufacture with their little air-cooled "peoples-wagon" designed by Ferdinand Porsche pre-war, and Graham purchased the second one off the assembly line in 1947, chassis No. VOLK/ 203 for £160, which he took back to the Island with him when his final "tour of duty" ended in 1948. The VW was a better buy than the Triumph mentioned above by Raymond Baxter; Graham was never happy with it, but managed to pass it on at a profit. Any form of nearly-new vehicles were in short supply in Britain for many years after the war when the bulk of new vehicle output was destined for the export markets.

Although his riding days were drawing to a close by this time and he was operating in Germany as a civilian, he obtained permission to enter a team from the B.A.O.R. in the 1948 International Six Days Trial, based that year at San Remo. His team consisted of Sgt. Hanson, R.E.M.E., Sgt. Ward, R.A.C. and Pte. Hall. He persuaded the powers-to-be to run a series of off-road trials in Germany, similar to those he instigated during the war. These proved a hit with the bored bike riding members of the Armed Forces in Germany, large numbers of whom were still required to be based on foreign soil long after the war had ended.

The Beetle clocked up well over 100,000 miles in Germany and back on the Island, still

The first Volkswagen on British soil. Graham with Edgar Hamill,
later to be the Island's first VW dealer

on its original engine. In the early post-war years, wherever he parked the VW on the Island it was mobbed by curious Manxmen who had never seen such a vehicle, its flowing lines sharply contrasting with the pre-war upright saloons that most still used. Volkswagen presented Graham with a tie-pin and certificate in recognition of the longevity of the car. Not a week after clocking up the magic mileage, it was nearly lost in a fiery inferno. Brother-in-law Bill Penny loaded a bale of straw onto the rear seat - fodder for the pigs Graham was keeping, the seat moved and shorted the battery out.

Returning to an Island home at Glen Maye, his return to commerce and a civilian way of life was assisted by a wartime colleague who had connections with the Marley Tile Co. In 1950 he formed the Douglas firm of J. Graham Oates, initially just selling the range of Marley roof tiles. The firm expanded into the largest supplier and fitter of roofing and flooring tiles, it changed hands but is no longer in the roofing market.

By now Graham was no longer a full-time rider, but he was as keen as ever to assist motorcycling in any capacity. Still a member of the Peveril Club, he assisted for many years in the running of the Isle of Man Grand National Scramble. This was firstly held near Windy Corner, but latterly the venue was moved to Douglas Head.

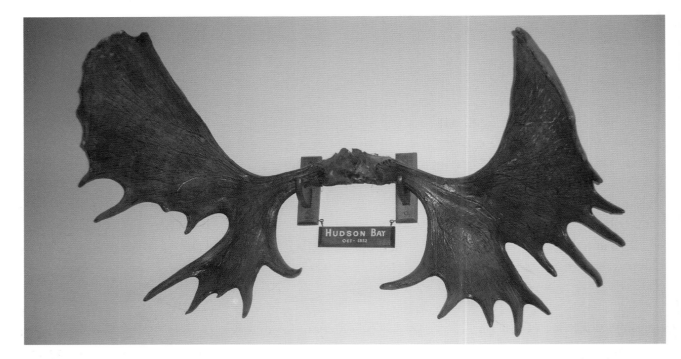

Around 1950 Betty bought a plot of land on Clay Head, Baldrine and Graham consructed a dwelling there. This was named 'Moose Lodge' and to this day the hall is graced by a enormous set of antlers from a moose that Graham bagged on his way to Churchill.

His interest in sidecar competitions led him to help instigate the sidecar class in the Manx National Two Day Trial in 1962 in collaboration with another ex-competitor John Catchpole. The Manx Two Day is still a classic event in the trials calendar, held on the weekend before the Manx Grand Prix races in September. The sidecar class still competes for the J.

Terry Moore (Velocette Viceroy) waits to be given the start signal by Graham at the 1967 Scooter Rally

Graham Oates Trophy for best sidecar performance. Appropriately, it was Ariel riding all-rounder Ron Langston who was the inaugural winner.

The British Empire Trophy car race was last held in the Island in 1953, and in the local press Graham advocated a longer race, possibly on the Mountain Circuit. If this was not feasible, he wrote, why not run it on a 15 mile triangular course starting at St. Johns, turning left at Ballacraine, left again in the outskirts of Kirk Michael and through to Peel, where another left would take the competitors back to St. Johns. This was, of course, the route of the original TT circuit used from 1907 to 1910. However, nothing ever came of this plan.

Through his contacts at the BBC, mainly Raymond Baxter, he was invited to assist as timekeeper with the live outside broadcast of the TT and Manx Grand Prix races on the North of England Home Service. In 1953 he was stationed at Parliament Square, helping a fledgling Murray Walker, whilst Murray's father, TT winner Graham Walker, was principal commentator at the Grandstand.

A founding member of the Manx section of the Vintage Motor Cycle Club, Graham helped the section persuade the parent club that there was a sufficient demand for a Vintage Rally during TT week. The first was organised for 1956 with Graham carrying out the start duties, flagging away the field from St. Johns, the original start to the TT in 1907, thus commencing a traditional event that carries on as one of the TT festival's most enduring and popular assemblies.

Graham fettles the troublesome Puch

In the late 50s the scooter boom was just starting. Many clubs had sprung up and interest in this new and more sanitised form of motorcycling was growing apace. There were many on the Island who recognised the potential for another week of two-wheeled sport, and they held the first Manx International Scooter Rally in 1957. Amongst the motorcyclists who took a hand in the running of the Scooter Week was Graham, now 58 years old. Harold Rowell was another who saw the potential of the scooter - especially as he was at the time running the Salisbury Garage in Fort Street, Douglas and sold Lambrettas.

A 24 hour reliability trial round the TT course had been run the year before, but the riders were unhappy with the speed schedules set. The question was - how could they assess the potential lap time for these machines in the '58 Rally. Solution - Harold Rowell (150 Lambretta), Edgar Cottier (75 DKW Hobby) and Graham (125 Puch) set to in October 1957 to ride the TT course for a 12 hour spell. These hardy enthusiasts started at 4 p.m. on a Saturday afternoon, intending to finish their run at 4 am on Sunday morning. The Puch gave trouble, so Graham was unable to complete the full distance. Cottier gave it best also, but Harold Rowell put in ten laps of the course at an average of over 31 mph. The information gained by this run helped the committee to make an ever greater success of the 1958 Scooter Week.

Graham was to confess later that the lightweight, small wheeled Puch was not exactly his idea of the perfect machine.

Even though he kept a most meticulous record of his riding achievements during the 30s, Graham very rarely spoke about them in later years. It took Wilf Halsall, then chairman of the local Vintage Club section, much persuasion before Graham would agree to give a talk at the Bowling Green Hotel, Douglas in 1963. The trouble was - there was so much to Graham's motorcycling life that he had barely got as far as the '39 International before the pub called 'time',

Allan Johnson of the Canadian Vintage Motorcycle Group has painted a concise pen portrait of Graham. *"I think J.G.O. must have been a very complex man. His enthusiasm for the motorcycle transcended all reason. He obviously enjoyed a challenge. He was shy and introspective (all fishermen are introspective) and then there is his oil painting hobby. But how could he have been shy when the 1932 trip was one of great promotion of motorcycles and subsequently he made up a slide show of his trips to show to various clubs and groups. Remembering that he was alone often in wilderness and struggling with a recalcitrant heavy sidecar outfit, the man must have had the stubbornness of an ox to go on day after day horsing those outfits over the rails. Can we say that he was one of the "bulldog breed", who once they set their mind to a task, however onerous, would carry it through.*

Certainly he was a complex figure"

Graham Oates passed away in 1972, aged 75. He was a slight man in stature, but undoubtedly a person with incredible strength of purpose and character. The loss of sight from his left eye so early in life made not a jot of difference to his skill, will, and determination to succeed, against all the odds.

Graham may have passed on, but his achievements should forever rank him amongst the highest in motor cyclings hall of fame.

In 2009 J. Graham Oates was inducted into the Canadian Motorcycle Hall of Fame.

Chapter 8

THE RACING CAREER OF GRAHAM OATES Jnr

The tall thin figure standing beneath the Madeira Drive arch contrasted sharply with the low black Lotus Europa at his feet. The silver beard and distinguished features were more the marks of an academic than a racing driver, yet there in the early morning fret stood a British champion.

Graham Oates, freshly crowned Leaders Sprint Champion, had no need to be in Brighton as he had clinched the title a fortnight earlier at Aintree. However, it was a measure of his sportsmanship that he had made the long journey south anyway to compete in last September's Speed Trials.

Born fifty nine years ago in Douglas on the Isle of Man, it was perhaps inevitable that Graham's motor sporting career should begin on two wheels. During the early sixties a 350cc BSA 'Gold Star' was road raced. A third place at Silverstone and the doubtful distinction of having Mike Hailwood ride around the outside of him at Oulton Park's Cascades are the lasting impressions of the Oates brave period.

A Gold medal from am International Scooter Rally run over the Manx TT course showed he could mix it with the Mods as well as Rockers, whilst a first foray into four-wheeled sport took the form of a few rallies at the wheel of an ex-works Riley 1.5.

Oates began sprinting in 1978 with a Lotus Europa twin-cam. The car had the dubious history, being what the motor trade's lower orders would describe as a 'two-halfer'. Two insurance write-offs provided the raw material, a £690 Europa with its

Graham Oates racing his Gold Star at Oulton Park

front swiped off, and a £150 example divested of its tail. Together they formed a fully trimmed BARC 'Marque' class contender, and using a sense of throttle control and balance honed on a racing motor cycle, Graham took a class win second time out, at Woodvale.

The black Lotus became a familiar and successful sight on the speed event scene, winning the 1985 BARC Hillclimb championship, and finished third in the 1986 Leaders Sprint series. High point was breaking Jeff Goodchild's 15-year old class record at Harewood in '85, low point was being disqualified at the same hill a year later for an innocent technical infringement, the Harewood Championship being lost as a result. Scariest moment was a suspension bolt breaking at Oulton Park when exiting Knicker Brook flat in fourth. The Lotus skimmed the barriers on both sides of the track.

For a serious bid for the Leaders Sprint title the car was completely rebuilt to 'Modsports' specification during 1987, a lightweight shell being mated to the original chassis, 1594cc engine, and Renault 17 gearbox. Eric Humphries' even lighter Lotus 7 kept the hospital biochemist out of the top placings in '88, although some fine dices ensued, but '89 and '90 produced third placings. Then, at last, with a little more weight shed and the motor opened out to 1800cc, the 1991 title was his.

With typical modesty the man from Formby attributes his success to sound preparation alone rather than driving skill, but over 300 class wins suggest otherwise, ably abetted by wife Adrienne and sons Andrew and Jeremy - plus gin and tonic, especially in Ireland and Scotland. All chassis, suspension set-ups and engines were self-built throughout his career.

In a racing career that continued through to 2008, he was RAC M.S.A. British Sprint Leaders Champion in 1991, 1992, 1994 and 1998.

The car was powered by a 1800cc twin-cam engine for the 1991-1994, events, supplanted by a 1800cc BDA Cosworth unit for 1998.

In 1992 he set a new Lotus record at the Brighton Speed Trials with self-built Lotus twin-cam engine, beating Tiff Needel of 'Top Gear' into second place; Tiff was driving a Lotus Esprit.

In his motor racing career he was:
Northern Speed champion five times
Lancashire A.C champion eight times
Nottingham F.T.D. champion
Yorkshire Speed champion

In 2008, on his retirement from competition, he was awarded the Peter Collins Trophy by the Lancashire Auto Club, in recognition of outstanding achievements in speed eventing.

Chapter 9

GRAHAM OATES AND ISLE OF MAN STAMPS

In 1993 Graham Oates and Bill Marshall featured on a set of stamps which were issued during the TT meeting. It features action from the 1933 International Six Days Trial.

A set of Manx stamps was issued to celebrate The International Polar Year 2007 - 2008. Graham Oates is featured on the day he entered Churchill on the Hudson Bay, October 4, 1932.